The Murder of Marilyn Monroe:
"Her Lips Were Sealed Until Now"

An Investigative – Educational Journal

We believe, we believe in good and evil, we choose good; we believe in right and wrong, we pick right; our cause is just, our enemies anywhere, they're all around us…some scary material out there; which brings us here, to the murder of Marilyn Monroe

Redefining History as We Know It

BY: T. Atencio & R. Gentillalli, M.Ed

Copyright © 2019 Tammy Atencio & Rick Gentillalli

All rights reserved

No copyrighted part of this book may be used or reproduced without expressed written permission of Tammy Atencio and Rick Gentillalli except in the case of brief quotations embodied in critical articles or reviews. Original documents and photographs, at your pleasure, can be confirmed in various archives, public YouTube, presidential libraries, foundations, and various intelligence agencies.

ISBN: 978-0-578-22802-0 (Hard Copy)

Library of Congress Control Number: 2019919479

Book Cover Design by Tammy Atencio and Rick Gentillalli

The information contained herein compiled using personal investigative interviews, the Freedom of Information Act, the Public Records Act. Including access to the public CIA's, FBI's FOIA Vault, critical articles, and public internet searches. We intended this to be an educational investigative journal used for public edification and educational institution's teachings. Complying with the Fair Use Act, with no intentional harm intended to any person or organization with a proprietary software check for plagiarism and correction of the same. Some information may be fictional with authentication to corroborate the findings.

Dedication

We dedicate this journal to our almighty God and his unique child, Marilyn Monroe, her fans, her family, and her friends.

And to people with Mental Illness, Substance Use, and Abuse issues, which is a plague that has crippled our society. The stigma has burdened individuals who experience these problems and prevents many from seeking help. As a result, bad things happen, and the flocks wonder, sometimes without hope. Marilyn Monroe was an example of Substance Abuse. Yet not adequately diagnosed with a mental illness, but rather the persona she exhibited while she was under the influence of barbiturates and alcohol one night, and stimulants the next morning.

To the Mother and Sister of T. Atencio, who are both deceased victims of substance use abusers.

To our men and woman in uniform, law enforcement, first responders, and the military armed forces – all of them who are serving and have served are heroes! Also, my son SSgt. Rick R. Gentillalli, for his sacrifice, while serving in the U.S.A.F., a flight crew member for the Supreme Allied Commander of NATO, killed on May 4, 2003.

Also, dedicated to the men and women working in the criminal justice system, the ethical, unwavering intelligence agencies, created to protect the United States of America and "We the People."

May you forever rest in peace - Marilyn Monroe

Introduction

LAPD and others KILLED MARILYN MONROE

Marilyn Monroe's life and death

There are no white hats or black hats- only grey; good & evil work together

The Central Intelligence Agency, well, they don't train farmers; they teach you how to deceive, role play, psychologically assess, sell, exploit – the black arts, not witchcraft, but rather a trade-craft! Marilyn was a potential security risk; read, and you will find out why!

You have just stepped through the looking glass, nothing you read will seem true- your perspective on right and wrong questioned - your trust in our government will waiver - your belief in the documents presented questionable…go with your gut feeling, it's about 95% accurate!

Marilyn Monroe, The Goddess – loved by many yet envied by more

Table of Contents

CHAPTER 1	The Beginning	11
CHAPTER 2	Marilyn Monroe – Murdered	15
CHAPTER 3	The Investigation	19
CHAPTER 4	False Information from LAPD	27
CHAPTER 5	Why Murder Marilyn	41
CHAPTER 6	The Players Involved	75
CHAPTER 7	Toxicology/Coroners Report/LAPD	97
CHAPTER 8	False Information, Wiretaps	123
CHAPTER 9	Who Murdered Marilyn	145
CHAPTER 10	Fascination and Legacy	159
CHAPTER 11	Continued Fascination	177
CHAPTER 12	Monroe's Unique Character	205
CHAPTER 13	Heartbeat of Hollywood	217
CHAPTER 14	JFK Assassination	233

CHAPTER 1

The Beginning

It was just another early evening field investigation, as we continued our search for additional clues and pieces of the puzzle. Our goal was to complete and corroborate the facts surrounding the murder of Marilyn Monroe. One early Friday evening, the temperature was in the high 60's as darkness set in; we parked several curbside houses away from the subject's home. Across the street was a grass field that was part of a fenced school ground. We looked at each other and decided to say a prayer before we walked to the door. We knocked on the door of a middle-class suburban single-family home in San Diego County. An older man in a wheelchair greeted us at the door. Yes, Yes, Yes – we found the man we were looking for, a retired Los Angeles Police Department, Organized Crime Intelligence Division Officer. He confirmed his name, former occupation, and also his involvement in the Marilyn Monroe Case. Ray said, in part, *"...we did a good job, it's something that had to be done, and we did it..."*

Our interview continued, and Ray confirmed things that only a participant in the murder would know. After the meeting, we left his residence and not a spoken word between my partner and me.

This surreal moment of one of the most interesting and 'once in a lifetime' interviews; we then left the house and neighborhood and parked about two or so miles away in a strip mall. We bought something to drink from a fast food joint, but our stomach had butterflies, and we weren't hungry. We learned and confirmed that Ray and his partner killed Marilyn!

We had to take several deep breaths as we sat there in silence, in awe, not believing what we have just learned from Ray. I told my partner, this is it, 'the smoking gun' so-to-speak, the last piece of evidence to say the real story of how Marilyn died by homicide. Oh my God, we left the City and drove to the beach – still in disbelief, we decided to sit on the beach and re-group taking in the ions and gentle sound from the ocean waves. All awhile, we were looking over our shoulders, thinking anything nefarious could happen. What if Ray called the CIA, FBI, or counterparts from the LAPD? Basically, what if he called his handler? We were sitting ducks, just waiting to be snuffed out because of the information we had just learned. After a short time by the ocean, we decided to drive back to our office. We realized that we were mentally exhausted from the overwhelming information we had just uncovered.

Finally, the truth revealed, and agencies disseminating false exculpatory information in Public Records Requests, and Freedom of Information Act requests from the CIA, FBI, Secret Service, LAPD, and the District Attorney's Office, proved to be a bunch of bullshit in effort to steer the public in different directions and make finding the truth almost impossible. Finally, disseminated to prove once and for all, 'Marilyn Monroe was snuffed - murdered,' and SHE DID NOT commit, as the Coroner stated on her death certificate, "…Probable Suicide…"

It's ironic how 'the' Marilyn Monroe Murder cover-up, way back in 1962, is very similar to what is happening today. With continued government cover-ups, murders, false flag operations and agencies with rogue agents operating in a manner that they are untouchable. Horrifying, yet we were on a mission to seek justice for Marilyn. The problem addressed, at least our agency is doing the best we can, with the information we uncovered. Today our Government calls murder, "collateral damage," for the protection of the United States of America. They also use other catchy, flashy phrases, to make things seem ok to the public and also that killing someone is acceptable. Let's face it, as time goes by, people dying, being murdered or committing suicide, like officials convince the public, are acceptable and done for the good of humanity and the United States of America! No, it isn't! In life, it's not believed to be this way. Follow our path in this exciting journey, and we will guide you through the lies and deception presented by our government to convince the public that Marilyn Monroe committed 'Probable Suicide.' And really, what the heck is probable suicide?

Keep an open mind, and this journey will take you into the deep state and their protection of the Democratic, Republican, and Socialist party – just like it is today! Also, to help you understand why disinformation serves to distract people from making the connections that lie at the heart of deception -

A few things to think about – **Elvis Presley**, Born January 8, 1935, Died August 16, 1977, cause of death: Cardiac Arrhythmia? Not from an overdose after he took his third packet of drugs from his assistant because he had trouble sleeping; died in the bathroom, yet the doctors claimed Cardiac Arrhythmia.

Michael Jackson, born August 29, 1958, died June 25, 2009; cause of death, Cardiac Arrest, from acute propofol & benzodiazepine intoxication?

Prince, born June 7, 1958, died April 21, 2016, cause of death "Accidental" fentanyl overdose?

Why are the above accidental deaths determined to be Cardiac Arrhythmia, Cardiac Arrest, and unintentional overdose? Common sense helps us gain entry into the corrupt J. Edgar Hoover FBI, Chief William Parker LAPD, the secret LAPD OCID hitmen, and James Angleton, Chief of CIA Counterintelligence.

So let's begin our path to the truth, together, in this mesmerizing presentation of facts to finally, once and for all, close the case of the Marilyn Monroe Murder at 12305 5th Helena Dr., Brentwood, CA. 90049

CHAPTER 2

Marilyn Monroe - Murdered

Several years ago, a retired intelligence operative (IO), joined the newly created volunteer public commission, where I was also a member. This secretive, knowledgeable, honest, former intelligence officer took a lead position immediately. Around the first time I met him, he told our team he was in the movie "Olympus Has Fallen." He played an essential part in the film, and he was also a technical advisor on the film. As time went on, we became friends, in most part, because he trusted me, and also I took an interest in his background and understood his conveyance of thoughts. He is a very smart man and was trained by the best and remained on the Good Guys team up to this day. The retired intelligence officer told us he was currently working as an investigator on a movie or documentary which focused on the last three days of Marilyn's life. He also said, point-blank, *"…Marilyn Monroe was murdered…"* and he knew this for a fact.

The intelligence organization he worked for many years ago was aware of this. He had full knowledge of it; however, he could not divulge who told him; this sparked our interest! This author has worked on twelve State Death Penalty cases, as a Federal Criminal Investigator for the United States Courts. The cases climbed the ladder to the District Court level for an appeal, and re-investigation. As a result, this sort of situation caught my eyes; I was hooked and wanted to learn more.

Additionally, the other author is a longtime fan of Marilyn Monroe and had a vested interest in finding the truth. Our agency delved into the investigation by sorting through every document available. Sending out FOIA and PRA requests to numerous agencies, we also reviewed every video available and reviewed innumerable books related to Marilyn Monroe's death.

As time went on, we suspected who he (IO) really worked for, another three-letter US Governmental agency, and the information from this intelligence agency was always 99.9% credible. They are the best intelligence agency in the world. The movie crew that our friend was currently working with contacted us on numerous occasions and attempted to solicit information with nothing in return.

We exchanged some information when we met the crew and learned they knew very little about the LAPD intelligence unit or cold case murders. Time passed, and we continued our investigation, interviewed numerous people both in State and out of state, and learned new things almost every week.

We learned, in part, how Marilyn was murdered, but the movie crew didn't want to believe us, 'the truth that we discovered that is.' The movie crew listened to want-to-be investigative journalists who didn't know about the investigation, homicides, or cold case murders. The Producer and Co-Executive Producer had great interest but did not believe us, insisting on the theory with Marilyn died as a result of an "accidental overdose."

They even went so far as to say the people we interviewed had to take a lie detector test. A lie detector test? Come on, how ignorant can you be as a producer to request interviewed individuals to take a lie detector test. I explained that this was problematic, and we would corroborate everything independently with other witnesses, documents, recordings, or other methods.

Thank God we never signed a contract with the movie crew, and from what I understand, several other investigators did not sign a contract. Yet, they have the rights to the movie through the actors guild – not sure about this, though.

Our quest for the truth and fact-finding expedition turned out to be an enormous chore. We ran across a retired LAPD Organized Crime Intelligence Division Officer who has a wealth of knowledge of the Marilyn Monroe Murder. After we befriended him, he told us Fred Otash was one of his snitches in the Los Angeles area (more about this later.) He shared a lot of information with us, yet kept a lot to himself. He is a sincere and honorable man with a quest for the truth. After I read a book authored by him, we concluded he might have a file or copy of some sort of related material on Marilyn Monroe. He also laid out the structure of the OCID, which in part, is in his book. We knew that he would have a wealth of information, and we took a chance to contact him. We learned the information presented to us and also, in part, how it happened. As we were leaving another state driving back to California, we received a phone call from the retired OCID Intelligence Officer. We pulled over and spoke with him for at least two hours on the side of the highway. It was during this phone call that we became friends, in which he took a great interest in finding the truth and also what we had learned as well as our contact with him.

He told us directly that Marilyn Monroe was murdered. The OCID officer implied that he 'may' have confidential information, including reports that said the same. He also may have read Marilyn's ledger (diary) and told us Marilyn was a decent writer and a smart woman. He implied, at least in our subjective belief, that he has the entire Marilyn Monroe file that includes transcripts of the recording of the night she was murdered. He received this file from a friend around the same time he was forced to retire. In part, because someone shot at Mike on numerous occasions, yes, this is in his book – possibly by the rouge OCID police officers whom he pissed off and betrayed their trust because of his honesty.

Since then, we have kept in contact with this wonderful, honest man. We compiled our list of OCID Operatives who were around during the time Marilyn was killed, which included, unbeknown to us, the two Intel officers who participated in her murder. The LAPD Intelligence Officer never told us any information about our OCID list.

So here we are, in 2015, we have two independent intelligence officers telling us Marilyn Monroe was murdered. Both of them are credible, worked for different agencies, did not know each other, honest to a fault, very smart, and believe in the good guy winning. Even with this said, neither one told us who killed Marilyn Monroe – leaving it up to us to find the facts and truth.

Summers, the author of Goddess: The Secret Lives of Marilyn Monroe, noted: "Both the forensic work and the police investigations were hopelessly flawed," Summers" said.

His fellow Marilyn Monroe biographers agree. "…One of the problems with this whole case is that there are so many conflicting stories..," said Spada. Michael Selsman, Monroe's last press agent and author of 'All Is Vanity,' was more direct. "No one knows the truth," he said. "No one will ever know the truth." In part, these are the same words the assassin told us when we interviewed him, a bit ironic isn't it; however, the truth revealed! *"Her Lips Were Sealed Until Now!"*

Well, we uncovered the truth, and the truth is known. Just follow the yellow brick road, and read a whole bunch of authenticated documents from the CIA, FBI and LAPD OCID. All put together in a manner that will leave you a bit perturbed at our government and their quest to silence the murder of Marilyn Monroe for national security? Or was it for political protection?

Happy reading, and please keep an open mind and remember that what happened back in 1962, is happening right now, with our excellent administration and their fight against the deep state, corrupt agencies, MSM news, and evildoers.

CHAPTER 3

The Investigation

We began more thorough research by watching YouTube videos and extracting things that made sense, including interviews and other bits of information. We came across a retired Los Angeles Police Officer, Organized Crime Intelligence Division, who gives the game away on LAPD when he wrote a book about the LAPD Elite Spy Network. Okay, we know, he has been mentioned - there was an attempt on his life; however, he had information that protected him from being killed. He was mentioned in Chapter 1 and discussed herein again.

Since then, we have kept in contact with Mike. We compiled our list of OCID Operatives who were around during the time Marilyn was killed, which included unknown to us, the two Intel officers who participated in her murder. Mike never told us any information about our OCID list. Fast forward, when we uncovered which officers were involved and what they did, the only reply from Mike was "good job."

DANIEL STEWART – LAPD OCID
(Married Peter Lawford's Widow- more to come)

Upon our early reviewing of YouTube videos, we came across one video where Dan has interviewed on the television program Hardcopy. Our initial review at that time didn't mean a whole lot. As time passed, we realized the importance that Dan, the LAPD OCID officer, really was an intricate part of the investigation.

HARDCOPY – 1992 Investigation into the death of MARILYN MONROE 3/4 (YouTube)

Dan said, *"...I was called out on a homicide investigation, and it was Robert Kennedy that was killed when I got down to the hospital. The officers in charge were the intelligence division officers, and they said this is really weird (Officer Dan says "Hello Ray") because they'd been watching Robert and Jack at Marilyn's place..."* (NARRATOR: THE CONVERSATION TURNED TO BOBBY AND MARILYN'S LAST NIGHT, BOBBY WAS UNDER SURVEILLANCE BY THE LAPD) Dan continued stating, *"...they picked him up, I think Santa Monica airport, followed him, took him up to Marilyn's took him back to the airport later that night when he left town..."*

As you can see from above, a critical name appears – RAY – this will all come together soon...

After locating Dan, we first interviewed him at his home in Rancho Mirage, CA on July 29, 2016, at approximately 6:00 p.m. Dan did come to the enclosed iron front gate and spoke with us. In part, we asked him if he recalled the two intelligence officers, related to Bobby's murder, at the hospital when he arrived, he paused, and said: "they're all dead." We said, "the OCID Officers," he said "yes," Dan said; he also worked Intel, and he is the only one standing upright. Dan also said he guarded Kennedy's door at hotels when they would have flings with women. We questioned the accuracy of a few books out there, no subjective reply so we exchanged business cards. Dan said, *"I really don't talk about this - let me make some calls and get back to you."* Dan offered to tell about the holes in the wall regarding the Kennedy assassination; he said, the holes were just nails according to Dan. Not what we wanted to hear. Dan also said he knew Fred Otash very well, *"...he worked for Spindel and Marilyn Monroe's house was wired by Otash, LAPD, FBI, Hoffa, the CIA and it looked like a telephone company had wired it. In the old days, it was easy..."* We asked Dan about Ray Strait's credibility, and Dan said NOTHING. Assuring us that after he checks us out, he will get back with us. An important fact, as we were leaving the house, Dan spontaneously turned back around and said: "by the way, the tapes still exist."

On January 4, 2017, we made a second attempt to interview Dan at the same home as before. He greeted us respectfully and said, *"...I remember you from before..."* he also confirmed that OCID officer Bill Jordan (deceased) was his partner. At the time, they protected the Kennedy's and other dignitaries, he went on to say – *"...but I have nothing to say, I'll talk to you later..."*

Within moments, Patricia, his wife, and Actor Peter Lawford's widow, opened the door and yelled: "get the hell out of here!" Dan added, "well, I might be talking to you later."

RAY CHARLES CADENA – LAPD OCID

After researching OCID officers, we could only find one Ray from the list. It turned out to be Ray Cadena. After many hours of researching, we determined that Ray Cadena lived in Santee, CA, and was retired from LAPD OCID. Ray was mentioned in reports and also the person Dan referred to in his HARDCOPY interview. We went to his home in Santee, CA, and approached the door at about 6:00 p.m. on November 14, 2016. We had a visible tape recorder openly in our hand and stood on the front porch where the mailbox was. Ray opened the screen door after several knocks and confirmed his identity. After introductions, he was reluctant to talk about Marilyn Monroe the first thing he said was "…how did you find me, no one has ever spoken with me about this…"

The transcript will be presented to the reader later- here are some highlights:

"…you got the right, Ray Cadena, I was in work there, I worked Intelligence division for 12 years, and I don't want to have a thing to do with you…"

"…you don't want the true stuff coming out, and people all over this country do not want it, the true stuff coming out…"

"…we did a good job, it's something that had to be done, and we did it…"

This will all come together with official documents and corroboration to give Marilyn the finality of changing her death certificate to "Homicide." We have to convince the Los Angeles County District Attorney or the State Attorney General to use our information, convene a Grand Jury, and come back with a murder conspiracy charge. Most everyone is dead or will be by the time this is complete; therefore, no one will go to jail; however, the truth will be told!

RAYMOND "Rusty" STRAIT– AUTHOR

Through our research, we came across the name Raymond a.k.a. "Rusty." We utilized our databases in hopes that he would still be alive and willing to speak with us. To our surprise, he is still alive and lives in a city we are close too. Rusty was 90 years old when we met, and is now 95 years old; Bless this man, he looks 70 and moves around like a 40-year-old. He has authored many books and just listening to him, if you wrote down his one liner's, you would have another book – Great friend and wonderful man! We met Rusty towards the onset of our investigation when we were involved with a movie production company. We've met with Rusty several times at a local restaurant, where we addressed our intentions and interest in him. We befriended each other, and to this day, we still speak occasionally. There are many YouTube videos of Rusty out there where he speaks of his very close friend Fred Otash, and the things Rusty heard the night Marilyn died.

Ray states that Otash asked him in the late '70s to hold onto a box and store it for him; Ray told us he never opened the box. Almost ten years later, around 1986, Fred Otash asked Ray to bring the box to Palm Springs, which we later learned was Dan's house. It was in the late 1980s that "Rusty" and Fred Otash listened to many hours of the tapes at Dan's home. Rusty says it was in December, around the Christmas tree, the two of them were drinking eggnog while listening to the recordings.

We interviewed Ray on video on October 31, 2016. The interview was over 1 hour long, and we have it preserved; however, it is too long to transcribe. Also, the version that Ray told us is not exactly what we've seen on YouTube videos. We might be speculating about him being reluctant to give us all the information, even though we're friends. His testimony will be preserved, on the old archive videos and our video. Of importance, Ray talks about hearing someone say, "…be careful with the needle…" the needle – Keep reading as the plot thickens, and you will find out who used the "needle" and for what…

Here are some highlights that may not have surfaced in the past

"*...the Kennedy's (Joe) put $250,000.00 in an account to pay off anyone who stood in the way of the Kennedy brothers' political agenda...*" Rusty stated, after the murder of Marilyn Monroe, Fred Otash received $100,000.00, and the two other persons, who we believe to be Robert Kennedy's bodyguards, both LAPD OCID officers, as well as on the CIA's payroll, as assets, were paid $75,000.00 each. Their names and what they did are detailed in this book. Including OCID records corroborating who they are and identifying the "Ray," telling us what they did the night of Marilyn's Murder!

Rusty also told us that "*...as Fred Otash was leaving Marilyn's house the early morning of August 5, 1962, after the clean-up, he crossed paths with LAPD Sargent Clemmons and said "hello..."* No one else knows this except Otash, Clemmons, and Rusty – and Fred told him this the night they listened to the tapes together.

Yet, more importantly, Raymond "Rusty" Strait told what he heard while listening to the tapes that they played at Dan's home. It happened in the presence of Fred Otash, both to us on video and the YouTube "**The Missing Evidence: The Death of Marilyn Monroe**." According to a constructed time-line about 2:30 p.m. on August 4, 1962, Bobby Kennedy arrived at Marilyn's home with his brother-in-law Peter Lawford – then Rusty went on to state "*...First I heard on the tape, that the housekeeper let him in, she said, oh Mr. Kennedy, she's been sleeping, and he said, well I need to talk to her! On the tapes, I heard Robert Kennedy, the first time he came to Marilyn's house, was early in the afternoon, and it was a very amicable visit, they were having a good time drinking, and I think they were doing a little bit of smooching, it sounded like smooching, but you know, sounds can be deceiving...*"; Milo Spirilio, one of Fred Otash's operatives said: "*...and then when it picks up again in the living room, that He had to leave her, that too many people were watching them, Hoover, the FBI, Hoffa, and she was never to call him again, and it was Marilyn heard on the tape ordering him out of the house, she was screaming...*" as Rusty states he heard Marilyn say: "*...get the hell out of my house...*" - That was Marilyn! So Kennedy and Lawford leave! Rusty went on to say – "*...she knew too much,* *and made too many threats, and whether or not she would have followed through with them, they couldn't risk it..."*

According to the tapes and interviews cited by biographer Richard Buskin, at approximately 9:45 p.m., eyewitnesses saw Kennedy return, Marilyn was on the phone in her bedroom with Screenwriter and Director Jose Balanos, who since died June 11, 1994. Jose was Marilyn's escort at the 1962 Golden Globe Awards. Also, the intelligence officers recorded this phone call. On the call, Marilyn told Jose about the UFO story, H-bomb testing, Cuba's Castro assignation plot, and other things that JFK told her during pillow talk.

Marilyn heard some noise from the guest cottage, so she told Jose, *"...I'll be back..."* I'm going to check this out; however, she never returned to finish her conversation with Jose.

Rusty heard, on the tapes, Kennedy and two of his aids; Kennedy's LAPD OCID/CIA bodyguards searching for something in the guest house, Peter Lawford was also there with Bobby: Rusty states: *"...so Marilyn comes into the scene, and you could hear her, and she's been drinking, and her voice was slurred; she wanted to know, what are you back here for, I thought you were leaving, and she had a conversation and she said all you people do is use me, all you want to do is use me you don't care about me, you just want to use me, and I'm tired of being used – those were her exact words- I'm tired of being used, and let me tell you something buster, what I know would make the headlines, and Bobby Kennedy told her, you know, you better keep your mouth shut if you know what's good for you 'I know what's good for me, I'm Marilyn Monroe, and you're not fucking with some extra here' he said I know who I'm dealing with, but you don't know who you are dealing with..."*

Then Otash heard, according to Richard Buskin, Bobby says, give her something to calm her down, which is when things turned to the dark side of the story! Rusty said, *"...you could hear them smother her, you two be careful with the pillow, ah, watch out for the shots, and I'm not sure if that was someone giving a shot, but it was obvious that she was being smothered..."*

Around 10:30 p.m., Eunice Murray returns home with the handyman and sees Marilyn comatose – she contacted Dr. Ralph Greenson. Dr. Greenson, in turn, called Arthur Jacobs, Marilyn's publicist, who handled Marilyn's press relations, and he was at the Hollywood Bowl with his wife, Natalie. Natalie, interviewed by **Hardcopy – 1962 Investigation into the death of Marilyn Monroe 2/4** – she said: *"...I think it was midway way, approximately 10:00 – 1030,*

I cannot say of course I don't remember exactly, but during the performance, he received the news that she had, in fact, died, and I didn't see him for three days…"

Rusty's memory is incredible, and he's honest to a fault, most of the time. He was reluctant to give the name of the person working for Fred Otash, who was outside in a paneled truck listening to everything that was happening, in real-time, via the wiretap, the night Marilyn was injected - murdered. Rusty got into some trouble in the past for disclosing his name! Luckily this didn't matter because, after many hours of investigation, we found the name of the operative working for Otash, who also worked for the CIA. Not only was this recorded, but transcripts made from the recording.

CHAPTER 4

False Exculpatory Information from LAPD

Our agency's quest to gather intelligence from the key agency was to make a Public Records Request from the Los Angeles Police Department. I mean, let's face it; they were the first agency to receive a 911 call of death – yes, about 4 ½ to 5½ hours after Marilyn was injected - murdered.

This endeavor to obtain documents started around March 11, 2016, and on the fourth attempt, LAPD finally complied with our request. The next few pages will walk you through our efforts to gain access to Public Information – what the heck was the LAPD, afraid of? The email dated Thursday, April 14, 2016, was our fourth attempt, and finally, as noted in the letter dated June 15, 2016, both the letter and business check were mailed to LAPD for retrieval of the documents they had. Stemming from the information below with additional documents they provided and also provided for your reading pleasure for you to determine if LAPD was incompetent, lying, a conspirator in a cover-up, or just being, you know, LAPD. However, it's ironic that the two intelligence officers who participated in the murder were LAPD OCID officers. Gee, you think LAPD would have known – unless the OCID was so secretive that no one knew what or when they did what they did…even if it meant MURDER!

LAPD re-opens the Marilyn Monroe investigation in 1982 with the article here below and also provided to this writer from a Public Records Act request to LAPD – after about three failed attempts…

"…Police Open the Files on Marilyn: No Bombshells…"
September 24, 1985, |DAVID FREED | Times Staff Writer

Twenty-three years after actress Marilyn Monroe died of a drug overdose in her Brentwood home, the Los Angeles Police Department on Monday released what it said was its confidential file on the case.

A department spokesman said the file was made public to dispel lingering *"speculation, innuendo and out-and-out lies"* that Monroe was the victim of foul play.

"...She committed suicide by barbiturates; that is the reality, and there is nothing very special about it except for the fact that she was Marilyn Monroe..." said Police Chief Daryl F. Gates. *"...It's not a pretty story. It's very tragic..."*

The half-inch-thick internal file contains a little new information. It includes copies of a newspaper article on Monroe's death, an excerpt from a book on Monroe, telephone bills from the last months of her life, bills that her physician and drug store submitted to her estate, detectives' summaries from interviews with a handful of people who last saw or spoke with the blonde, 36-year-old sex symbol, and autopsy reports.

Former Los Angeles County Chief Medical Examiner Theodore J. Curphey concluded in 1962 that Monroe's death was *"caused by a self-administered overdose of sedative drugs and that the mode of death is probable suicide."* In an L.A. CO. D.A. memo dated August 18, 1982, DA investigator Al Tomich interviewed Dr. Curphy, who stated in part, *"...I'll be God damned if I'll get involved..."* referring to the Monroe investigation.

Gates said he decided to release the police file after receiving a request for the information from ABC's "20-20" television program, which reportedly plans to broadcast a report on Monroe's death this week.

Part of the file was censored *"to protect people's privacy,"* Gates said. Phone numbers from Monroe's last telephone bill were heavily redacted. Also, photos taken at the death scene were blacked out. *"But, at least, when (writers) come to us from now on, we can tell them that we have released everything we have on her,"* he said. Our take on what Gates said, sure, they released everything – what an out-and-out lie! Something few know is that Gates made copies of the (eavesdrop) Tapes and the transcripts of the night of the murder August 4, 1962. More on this with full names and more detailed information.

Gates said that the original file on Monroe's Aug. 5, 1962 death was destroyed in 1972, under a police regulation which requires that records ten years or older purged.

Chief Gates said that the file made public is a nearly complete duplicate of the one that detectives compiled in the weeks following Monroe's death. He said he had seen the original file and could not remember if anything was missing. (If Gates could answer from his grave, was he talking about the LAPD false exculpatory reports or the LAPD OCID reports?)

The file made public compiled during a 1975 investigation of Monroe's death by the department's Organized Crime Intelligence Division. That "reinvestigation" was ordered by then-Police Chief Ed Davis, in response to the publication of an article in Oui magazine that was critical of the Police Department's handling of the case, Gates said.

Copies of documents from the original file discovered in the personal archives of Thad Brown, a deceased former chief of detectives, the chief added.

The Oui article, which was rebutted in the file made public, said that Monroe was not suicidal. The story theorized that she had been injected with a lethal dose of drugs in the afternoon before her death. The article also theorized that Los Angeles police, in collusion with the Los Angeles County coroner's office, distorted evidence to protect then U.S. Atty. Gen. Robert F. Kennedy, with whom Monroe was rumored to have had a secret love affair.

Others, including a man who claimed to have been secretly married to Monroe, have asserted that Monroe was injected – murdered because of her association with Robert Kennedy and his knowledge of U.S. intelligence plots against Cuban leader Fidel Castro.

Spurred by those allegations, and charges that a former coroner's assistant pressured into signing a suicide death certification, the Los Angeles County district attorney's office in 1982 conducted its own three and 1/2-month investigations. It discounted theories that Monroe had been murdered and that the Police Department had covered it up.

"Based on the evidence available to us, it appears that her death could have been suicide or come as a result of an accidental drug overdose . . . ," said then-District Attorney John Van de Kamp, California's attorney general in 1982. *"...Permit me to express a faint hope that Marilyn Monroe is permitted to rest in peace..."*

Well, a couple of things are wrong with what Chief Gates said*: "...But, at least, when (writers) come to us from now on, we can tell them that we have released everything we have on her," he said..."* This statement is a straight out lie as told by the Chief – in fact, we will tell you about one of Chief Gates's personal friends, a retired LAPD officer who had a copy of the tape recording and transcript of the night Marilyn was injected - murdered. When Gates personal friend and co-worker passed away, his widow gave the "box of information" to LAPD because she was scared to have it in her possession. We missed getting it by a few hours or maybe a day – God Bless the widow, she had nothing to do with anything, and I'm not sure she even knew what she had handed over! LAPD Police Chief Beck was in-charge at this time; however, he never responded to our calls; then, he ups and retires – either because of the alleged affair he was having with a female Captain or looking to distance himself from LAPD and make bank on the tapes? We may never know!

Of interest, however not corroborated, in the LAPD vault for OCID files, there's allegedly a file labeled Marilyn Monroe that contains 723 pages – where are they? Hidden or destroyed because LAPD OCID officers participated in the act of murder and Chief Parker believed, if he covered it up, he would be the next FBI director, if and when, Robert Kennedy became president. Let's face it, Parker helped destroy or hide pertinent records that were exculpatory, and he had no problem doing it! If Chief Parker were alive – he should be prosecuted for conspiracy to commit murder and the cover-up of the same. No such luck!

Most, if not all, of the documents received from the Los Angeles Police Department via our PRA request, are useless garbage. On the next few pages are copies of the LAPD police reports provided to me from my PRA (5 total - attached.) There's also the fact that many people say that Robert Kennedy was not in Los Angeles on August 4, 1962, the evening he participated in the murder of Marilyn Monroe. So let's set this straight:

Mayor Sam Yorty of Los Angeles interviewed by Bill Bixby (**the Marilyn Monroe Files Live 1992 on video**) – Sam was the mayor in the summer of 1962 – *"...I asked my police liaison officer to get me a copy of the police file on the death of Marilyn Monroe. I was told there was no file! Also, Chief Parker told me that Bobby Kennedy was in Los Angeles the night Marilyn died..."*

Bill Bixby interviewed Beverly Hills Police Officer Lynn Franklin (**the Marilyn Monroe Files Live 1992 on video**), he said, a few minutes after midnight *"...I stopped a late-model Lincoln travailing in Beverly Hills East Bound on Olympic boulevard traveling 75 miles an hour in a 25 mile an hour zone; driving the car was Peter Lawford whom I have known for a number of years and seated in the front with him was a man who I later identified as Dr. Greenson, Marilyn Monroe's Psychiatrist, and in the back seat was the Attorney General Bobby Kennedy; I asked Peter Lawford why he was driving so fast, he looked over his shoulder at the Attorney*

General and said I'm trying to get him to the Hilton Hotel to pick-up his luggage so he could get out of town, and I shinned my flashlight in the Attorney General's face so I could recognize him; they appeared to be uptight like they were trying to get somewhere and doing 75 MPH in a 25 zone, but they were uptight. A few days later, I received information that Bobby Kennedy was not even in the area and he was in San Francisco, so I thought there was something wrong here so for my curiosity I went to the Hilton Hotel and checked out and found that he was registered there that particular night. I received a copy of the registration; a few days later the Chief called me into the station, and a two Secret Service guys were there, and they demanded a copy of the registration that I had picked up at the hotel, I said hey guys get your own this is mine – later, it came up missing from my files. I think it was a total cover-up, you see the Secret Service is sworn to protect the Attorney General and the President of the United States; not to expose them, they follow them around, and they know what is going on. At the time I pulled the vehicle over, I did not know Marilyn Monroe had been murdered, I didn't know until the next day afternoon when I started to come back to work, and then I started putting two and two together..."

Authors Patte Barham and Peter Brown – *"Marilyn: The Last Take"* interviewed by Bill Bixby (**the Marilyn Monroe Files Live 1992 on video**) said the term Probable Suicide was very crucial of Fox's collection of the $13,000,000.00 life insurance policy – direct 'provable' suicide would have negated a great deal of the insurance – especially the $10M policy with Continental Casualty; it was important for Fox, and as you know they had clout with Chief Parker and the Coroner Office, that this certificate read "Probable Suicide." Patte Barham said, "...she was snuffed - murdered, and it's the biggest cover-up of the century..."

ATTACHMENTS

Debra Green

Discovery Section

Martin Bland, Senior Management Analyst

Officer-in-Charge, Discovery Section

Legal Affairs Division

Below is a copy of my email sent to L.A.P.D. on April 14, 2016, regarding my CPRA request on the L.A.P.D. death file of Marilyn Monroe. This is my fourth request with each one adding new information to compel your office to comply with said request. The last request adds a very strong reason for your office to comply based on simple facts within the California Public Records Act (CPRA). It is possible you did not receive this email or it was somehow overlooked; and if so, I apologize in advance. However, I have not heard back from L.A.P.D. regarding the April 14, 2016 request, and if it will be honored or denied.

I can only hope there will not be any negative repercussions against me or my agency for the continued request for information.

Again, thank you in advance,

Rick Gentillalli, M.Ed., Th.D. (c)

Gentillalli & Associates
Criminal Investigators, CA PI 14248
P.O. Box 293
Murrieta, CA 92564
951 553 3195
www.ciiagency.com

Sent from Mail for Windows 10

From: Rick Gentillalli
Sent: Thursday, April 14, 2016 4:39 PM
To: discovery@lapd.lacity.org
Cc: ▮▮▮▮▮▮▮@yahoo.com; mayor.garcetti@lacity.org
Subject: 3rd response (denial) letter from L.A.P.D.

Martin Bland, Senior Management Analyst June 15, 2016

OIC, Discovery Section

Los Angeles Police Department

RE: 14.4 PRA – Marilyn Monroe

Mr. Martin Bland,

Thank you for your cooperation and timely response. Enclosed are a copy of your letter dated June 9, 2016, and a business check made payable to LAPD in the amount of $12.80. Please send the information to:

(Confidential secure site)

Investigator Gentillalli

Again, thanking you in advance,

Rick Gentillalli, M.Ed.

Criminal Investigator

Gentillalli & Associates, CA PI #14248

rick@ciiagency.com

LOS ANGELES POLICE DEPARTMENT

CHARLIE BECK
Chief of Police

ERIC GARCETTI
Mayor

P. O. Box 30158
Los Angeles, California 90030
Telephone: (213) 978-2100
TDD: (877) 275-5273
Reference Number: 14.4

June 9, 2016

Mr. Rick Gentillalli
Gentillalli & Associates
rick@ciiagency.com

Dear Mr. Gentillalli:

I have reviewed your supplemental California Public Records Act (the Act) request, dated May 7, 2016, for records regarding the investigation of the death of actress Marilyn Monroe.

Staff from the Los Angeles Police Department's (the Department) Records and Identification Division has located the report that was made public by the Department. I will provide you with a copy upon receipt of the duplication fee.

Please submit a check or money order in the amount of $12.80, made payable to the LAPD, and a copy of this letter to the Los Angeles Police Department - Discovery Section, 201 North Los Angeles Street, Space 301, Los Angeles, California 90012. If you have any questions regarding this correspondence, please contact Management Analyst Debra Green of the Discovery Section at (213) 978-2156.

Very truly yours,

CHARLIE BECK
Chief of Police

MARTIN BLAND, Senior Management Analyst
Officer-in-Charge, Discovery Section
Legal Affairs Division

AN EQUAL EMPLOYMENT OPPORTUNITY EMPLOYER
www.LAPDOnline.org
www.joinLAPD.com

EMPLOYEE'S REPORT

DR: Unknown

Police Reports on Marilyn Monroe Death

Date & Time Occurred: 8-5-62
Location of Occurrence: W.L.A.
Division of Occurrence: W.L.A.

Rank, Name, Assignment, Division: Lt. L. Selby, OIC, Homicide Special Sec., R.H.D.

Date & Time Reported: 8-27-74

At the request of Commander McCauley, an attempt was made to determine the number and type of police reports taken by this Department in connection with Marilyn Monroe's death which occurred in W.L.A. Div. on Aug. 5, 1962. Commander McCauley also requested we determine if any of these reports were still available at this time.

In this regard, Sgt. Sturgeon, O.I.C., R. & I. Div., was contacted and requested to make a search of R. & I. files in an attempt to locate any reports we may have. He stated he could locate no records pertaining to the 1962 death of Miss Monroe. He further stated that all original crime reports that are controlled by R. & I. Div. are destroyed after a 10-year retention period. All reports, file cards, and DR blotters are included in the destruction.

Note: Attached is a copy of correspondence dated Sept. 4, 1973, to Assistant Chief D. F. Gates from Assistant Chief D. H. Speck pertaining to the "retention and destruction of crime reports."

The files at R.H.D. were checked for any records of the death of Miss Monroe. This division has no such records.

Investigators contacted W.L.A. Div. and were informed that they had no crime reports in their files pertaining to Miss Monroe's death. It was further determined from present W.L.A. investigators that the original W.L.A. detective who handled that case was Sgt. R. E. Byron, now retired.

Mr. Byron was contacted ▓▓▓▓▓▓▓▓▓▓▓▓▓▓▓▓▓▓▓▓▓▓▓▓▓▓▓▓ of Miss Monroe's death. He stated he was called to the scene Lieuts. Gregoire and Armstrong also responded. Byron stated he completed a death report and believes that he classified it as "accidental." Byron believes that he subsequently made a follow-up report to the original death report but is not sure how that was classified.

Byron does not have copies of any of these reports nor does he know of any existing copies.

CONFIDENTIAL

Time Typed: 8-28-74 1010
Divn. Rptg.: RHD
Clerk: rc
Employee(s) Reporting: L. A. Murray
Ser. No.: 6692
Divn.: RHD

DEATH REPORT

DATE AND TIME REPORTED				
8-5-62		Possible Accidental		
DATE AND TIME DEATH OCCURRED	LOCATION OF OCCURRENCE			DR No.
8/5-62 03/3:35A	12305 Fifth Helena Drive			REPORTING DISTRICT 814
	LOCATION OF ORIGINAL ILLNESS OR INJURY	CITY	REPORTING DISTRICT	TYPE OF ORIGINAL REPORT
NAME OF DECEASED	RESIDENCE ADDRESS		CITY	BUSINESS ADDRESS
Monroe, Marilyn	"			
OCCUPATION	SEX	DESCENT	AGE	HEIGHT	WEIGHT	HAIR	EYES	BUILD	COMPLEXION
	Female	Caus	36	5-4½	115	Blnd	Blu		

OCCUPATION OF DECEASED: Actress
PROBABLE CAUSE OF DEATH: Possible accidental
DATE AND TIME DECEASED DISCOVERED: 8-5-62 3:30A
REMOVED BY: Westwood Mortuary
RELATIVE: Gladys Baker, (Mother)
PERSON REPORTING DEATH TO POLICE DEPARTMENT: Dr. Hyman Engelberg
NAME: Ralph S. Greenson, Dr. Hyman Engelberg

Deceased retired on 8-4-62, at about 8:00 P.M. at her apartment, 12305 Fifth Helena Drive, Brentwood. At about 3:30 A.M. 8-5-62 Mrs. Murray, the maid, observed a light on in the deceased's bedroom. The door being locked, and she being unable to get an answer, she called Dr. Ralph R. Greenson, 436 Roxbury Drive. Upon arrival he broke into the bedroom through the french window and found the deceased possibly dead. He then called Dr. Engelberg who pronounced her dead at 3:35 A.M.

(remainder illegible)

Los Angeles Police Department
FOLLOW-UP REPORT

THE CRIME: DEATH REPORT
DR: 62-509 463
DATE AND TIME OCCURRED: 8/5/62 CP/3:35A
DATE AND TIME OF THIS REPORT: 8-8-62 4:15P
LOCATION OF OCCURRENCE: 12305 Fifth Helena Dr.
NAME: MONROE, Marilyn

Upon reinterviewing both Dr. Ralph R. Greenson (Wit #1 and Dr. Hyman Engelberg (Wit #2) they both agree to the following time sequence of their actions.

Dr. Greenson received a phone call from Mrs Murray (reporting person) at 3:30A, 8-5-62 stating that she was unable to get into Miss Monroe's bedroom and the light was on. He told her to pound on the door and look in the window and call him back. At 3:35A, Mrs Murray called back and stated Miss Monroe was laying on the bed with the phone in her hand and looked strange. Dr. Greenson was dressed by this time, left for deceased residence which is about one mile away. He also told Mrs Murray to call Dr. Engelberg.

Dr. Greenson arrived at deceased house at about 3:40A. He broke the window pane and entered through the window and removed the phone from her hand.

Rigor Mortis had set in. At 3:50A, Dr. Engelberg arrived and pronounced Miss Monroe dead. The two doctors talked for a few moments. They both believe that it was about 4A when Dr. Engelberg called the Police Department.

A check with the Complaint Board and the Desk, indicates that the call was received at 4:25A. Miss Monroe's phone, GR 61893 has been checked and no toll calls were made during the hours of this occurrence. Phone number 472-4830 is being checked at the present time.

INTERVIEWING OFFICERS: R E BYRON 2730 WLA D

EMPLOYEE'S REPORT

RE-INTERVIEW OF PERSONS CLOSE TO MARILYN MONROE

Date & Time Occurred	Location of Occurrence	Division of Occurrence
August 8, 1962	Various	

G. H. ARMSTRONG, COMMANDER, WEST L. A. DETECTIVE DIVISION — 8-10-62 8:30A

DETAILS

The following is a resume of the interview conducted in an effort to obtain the times of various phone calls received by Miss Monroe on the evening of her death. All of the below times are estimations of the persons interviewed. None are able to state definite times as none checked the time of these calls.

MILTON RUDIN —

Mr. Rudin stated that on the evening of 8-4-62 his exchange received a call at 8:25P and that this call was relayed to him at 8:30P. The call was for him to call Milton Ebbins. At about 8:45P he called Mr. Ebbins who told him that he had received a call from Peter Lawford stating that Mr. Lawford had called Marilyn Monroe at her home and that while Mr. Lawford was talking to her, her voice seemed to "fade out" and when he attempted to call her back, the line was busy. Mr. Ebbins requested that Mr. Rudin call Miss Monroe and determine if everything was alright, or attempt to reach her doctor. At about 9P, Mr. Rudin called Miss Monroe and the phone was answered by Mrs. Murray. He inquired of her as to the physical well being of Miss Monroe and was assured by Mrs. Murray that Miss Monroe was alright. Believing that Miss Monroe was suffering from one of her despondent moments, Mr. Rudin dismissed the possibility of anything further being wrong.

MRS. EUNICE MURRAY —

Mrs. Murray stated that she had worked for Marilyn Monroe since November, 1961, that on the evening of 8-4-62 Miss Monroe had received a collect call from a Joe DiMaggio, Jr. at about 7:30P. Mrs. Murray said that at the time of this call coming in, Miss Monroe was in bed and possibly had been asleep. She took the call and after talking to Joe DiMaggio, Jr., she then made a call to Dr. Greenson and Mrs. Murray overheard her say, "Joe Jr. is not getting married, I'm so happy about this." Mrs. Murray states that from the tone of Miss Monroe's voice, she believed her to be in very good spirits. At about 9P, Mrs. Murray received a call from Mr. Rudin who inquired about Miss Monroe. Mr. Rudin did not talk to Miss Monroe. Mrs. Murray states that these are the only phone calls that she recalls receiving on this date.
Note: It is officers opinion that Mrs. Murray was vague and possibly evasive in answering questions pertaining to the activities of Miss Monroe during this time. It is not known whether this is, or is not intentional. During the interrogation of Joe DiMaggio, Jr., he indicated he had made three phone calls to the Monroe home, only one of which Mrs. Murray mentioned.

JOE DiMAGGIO — Miramar Hotel, Room 1035, Santa Monica

Mr. DiMaggio was informed of the rumor which quoted him as saying that

ITEM No.	QUAN.	PAGE No.	TYPE OF REPORT	BOOKING NUMBER	DR No.
		2	RE-INTERVIEWS		62-509 463

he would not invite Mr. Lawford to the funeral services because he could have saved Marilyn's life and didn't. Mr. DiMaggio denied this, stating that he had not talked to any member of the press, nor had he said such a thing to anyone who might have repeated it to the press. He stated that the decision to limit the number of people was a mutual agreement, decided upon in order to keep from hurting the feelings of many of Marilyn's friends who might be accidentally overlooked.

JOE DiMAGGIO, JR. - Miramar Hotel, Room 1035, Santa Monica

Joe DiMaggio, Jr. was in his father's suite and interviewed immediately after the above interview. He stated that he had placed three collect calls to Miss Monroe on 8-4-62 and that the first call was about 2P. He could overhear the operator talk to Miss Murray who informed the operator that Miss Monroe was not in. The second call was placed at approximately 4:30P and again was answered by Mrs. Murray, and again he was unable to contact Miss Monroe. The third call was placed at approximately 7P and on this occasion Mrs. Murray stated that she would see if Miss Monroe was available and in a few moments Miss Monroe came on the phone and he held a short conversation with her. During the conversation, he told Miss Monroe that he was not going to get married. The time of the last call is estimated to be 7P, as he states it was during the 6th or 7th innings of the Angels-Orioles baseball game in Baltimore.

PETER LAWFORD -

An attempt was made to contact Mr. Lawford, but officers were informed by his secretary that Mr. Lawford had taken an airplane at 1P, 8-6-62. It is unknown at this time the exact destination, however his secretary stated that she did expect to hear from him and that she would request that he contact this Department at his earliest convenience.

R. E. Byron #2730
W.L.A. Detectives

CHAPTER 5

Why Murder Marilyn

One of the questions we promised to answer, at least to the best of our knowledge based on evidence and facts, "why" was Marilyn murdered? Several powerful implications would promote a reason for her demise. First, is her connection to communism – yes communism and tendency to be attracted to leftist? Also, Marilyn's friendship with Mafia figures and even alleged sexual relationships with them – I say them because there was more than one!

The other is her connection to John Kennedy, the President of the United States, and his brother Robert Kennedy, at the time, the United States Attorney General. What a dichotomy of characters as one is opposite the other, or at least one would think – but were they? Oh, and don't forget the life insurance policy Fox studios had on her.

THE MAFIA

Marilyn had a strong attraction and friendship with Frank Sinatra. It's alleged she likely had at least one sexual encounter with him and possibly more than one. Frank entertained the MOB in more ways than others. He was their friend along with the rest of the Rat Pack. More dangerous was the last weekend of July 1962, when Marilyn went to the Cal-Neva lodge with her friends, Peter Lawford and his wife, Patricia **(ATTACHED)**. At the Lodge was Singer Buddy Greco, who was the headliner act; Buddy said in an interview on video **(The Missing Evidence: the death of Marilyn Monroe - YouTube)** – *"...Frank Sinatra was there, and Sandy was there, Sam Giancana was there, Tony Lima, the list just went on and on and on..."* While at the Lodge, Marilyn, in an angry rant, vowed to have a press conference to expose the Kennedy's. Sirens went off, so-to-speak, and as you can imagine, all hell broke out all over the place. Most everyone knew when Marilyn was highly intoxicated, with both liquor and barbiturates, Sam

Giancana, the Mafia Boss, had sex with her. Allegedly photos were taken of him straddling her doggie style (the negative of one photo exists). Sam had his way with her without her consent! Giancana, after that, made a statement (un-confirmed) that she was a lousy fuck! Giancana's reason for meeting Marilyn at the lodge was to convince her not to spill the beans on the Kennedy's – in exchange, both John and Bobby Kennedy would back off of the prosecution of the Mob Boss. Both sides are total degenerate dirtbags! There are no black hats and white hats – There're all in bed together.

COMMUNISM

We see the communism started rising with Marilyn Monroe when she married play writer Arthur Miller in 1956. As the United States House Committee put it, "they wanted Miller to testify on alleged links with some 29 organizations, cited as Communist fronts, by the House Committee on Un-American Activities, or the United States Attorney General." He was an apparent Communist sympathizer, according to the U.S. Government, and they believed he could be a high-level security threat! Now you don't have to believe us, so attached are FBI documents **with four pages - attached, dated September 27, 1956**, for your confirmation? If you still have doubts, go to the FBI Vault under the FOIA release program and read it there. Since Miller was on his honeymoon with Marilyn during the committee hearings, he did not appear and cited for contempt. Marilyn's name is throughout the FBI document for your reading pleasure and corroboration of the facts stated.

Regarding Marilyn and her links to communism, it is another four-page FBI document dated **March 6, 1962 – attached – 4 pages,** just five months before she was eliminated. It states she went to Mexico on vacation the last few weeks in February, and she associated very closely with present or past members of the Communist Party - also, associates who shared sympathy for Communism and the Soviet Union. Of interest to the FBI was Ms. Monroe's association with Frederick Vanderbilt Field. Records revealed that Marilyn, accompanied by her press-agent, also her hairdresser, and her interior decorator – the decorator, was named Eunice Churchill in the FBI report. The previously mentioned memo on page 2-3 states, in part: *"...The subject arrived* *in Mexico on 2/19/62 from Miami. Her entry into Mexico reportedly was arranged by Frank Sinatra through former President Miguel Aleman. It became clear that a relationship was developing between subject and Field, and considerable concern was expressed over this by various members of the ACGM, such as MAY BROOKS (Bufile 100-414864), CHARLES SMOLIKOFF (Bufile 100-12632), and RUTH CONDE, aka RUTH ASHMORE BROWN. CHARLES SMOLIKOFF said that FIELD was completely infatuated with MONROE..."* Because of this, they were under constant FBI surveillance, so the memorandum was sent directly to J. Edgar Hoover, Director of the FBI.

A little bit about Eunice Churchill, a.k.a. Eunice Murray (the housekeeper allegedly hired by Dr. Greenson), a.k.a. Eunice Porter, a.k.a. Eunice Guthrie – she worked, or should I say, was paid by Dr. Greenson and the FBI to report back about Marilyn Monroe. Eunice was also on Marilyn's payroll as a housekeeper; as you can see, the FBI even tried to cover who she was by calling her 'Eunice Churchill' in the 1962 memo. Eunice Murray was a hired spy!

Initially, Ms. Eunice Murray, recruited by Dr. Milton Wexler, Psychologist, (California license number 374,) an associate of Dr. Ralph Greenson, M.D. (California license number A6753,) born Romeo Samuel Greenschpoon, was to watch the movement of Marilyn Monroe and report back to Dr. Greenson, Numerous other FBI memos depict Marilyn's involvement with the communist, leftist party, and the same documented and stored in the FBI FOIA vault. Feel free to peruse the vault to confirm our findings. More on good old Dr. Greenson further on in this book – I mean, let's face it; he was there the night the murder occurred. Marilyn was considered a national security risk by the CIA and FBI.

The KENNEDY'S

Regarding the Kennedy's, here's the juicy stuff – no pun intended. Robert Kennedy began enjoying Marilyn's company at Peter Lawford's house, who was married to Kennedy's sister, Pat, in the latter part of 1961. Robert had several rendezvous with Marilyn even up until the night she was injected – murdered, on August 4, 1962. There are numerous books out that have alleged dates of the encounters; however, we could not confirm this with reliable corroborated documentation. Unfortunately, false exculpatory information documented to confuse the public and above-board officials.

On March 24, 1962, JFK allegedly spent the weekend with Marilyn at Bing Crosby's home in Palm Springs. Marilyn sang at JFK's birthday party in May 1962, both well documented in public and confidential reports.

As a result of the pillow talk between Marilyn and Robert & Marilyn and Jack, she knew way too much – she kept a diary of most of the conversations with the brothers. There was also a wiretap summary between Dorothy Kilgallan and Howard Rothberg.

This writer tried to determine the authenticity of the Dorothy Kilgallan and Howard Rothberg wiretap conversation that was signed by James Jesus Angleton, CIA Chief of Counterintelligence, from 1954 to 1975. He was a Yale undergraduate and briefly studied law at Harvard Law School but did not graduate. Angleton is known for the CIA projects - Enigma Code, Manhattan Project, and Operation CHAOS. On Christmas Eve 1974, Angleton resigned from the CIA because *"....the CIA was getting involved in 'police state activities..."* (Wikipedia.)

The CIA

Okay, back to the memo distributed August 3, 1962, one day before Marilyn was silenced - murdered. Allegedly, there was a wiretap where the conversation between Dorothy Kilgallen, an American journalist, and her friend Howard Rothberg recorded. For ease of reading here is a summary as best the authors can decipher (copy attached, received from the CIA):

CENTRAL INTELLIGENCE AGENCY
TOP SECRET NOT FOR PUBLICATION
COUNTRY: New York, US
SUBJECT: Marilyn Monroe

REPORT NO. [blacked out]
DATE DSTR: 3 August 1962
NO. PAGES: [blacked out]
REFERENCES: MOON DUST

MJ-12

Wiretap of a telephone conversation between reporter Dorothy Kilgallen and her close friend, Howard Rothberg (A); from a wiretap of telephone conversation of Marilyn Monroe and Attorney General Robert Kennedy (B). Appraisal of Content: [blacked out]

1. Rothberg discussed the apparent comeback of the subject with Kilgallen and the break up with the Kennedys. Rothberg told Kilgallen that Marilyn was attending Hollywood parties hosted by the "inner circle" among Hollywood's elite and was becoming the talk of the town again. Rothberg indicated in so many words that she had secrets to tell, no doubt arising from her trists with the President and the Attorney General. One such "secret" mentions the visit by the President at a secret airbase to inspect things from outer space. Kilgallen replied that she knew what might be the source of the visit. In the mid-fifties, Kilgallen learned of a secret effort by US and UK governments to identify the origins of crashed spacecraft and dead bodies from a British government official. Kilgallen believed the story might have come from the New Mexico story in the late forties. Kilgallen said that if the story is true, it will cause terrible embarrassment for Jack and his plans to have NASA put men on the moon.

2. The subject repeatedly called the Attorney General and complained about the way she was being ignored by the President and his brother.

3. The subject threatened to hold a press conference and would tell all.

4. The subject made reference to "bases" in Cuba and knew of the President's plan to kill Castro.

5. The subject made reference to her "diary of secrets" and what the newspapers would do with such disclosures.

MJ-12

The memo is signed by James Angleton, then CIA Chief for Counterintelligence. Above Angleton's signature appears a second Top Secret stamp.

Analysis of the memo is as follows:

1. Inspecting things from outer space? Unconfirmed sources state that the recovery of a 'flying disk bomb' near Los Alamos, New Mexico, on March 25, 1947, and of another 'disk-like object,' on May 28, 1947, near the White Sands Proving Grounds, were housed at the Sandia Laboratory. Additionally, the Roswell crash in 1947 allegedly included two aliens of which one was alive. In part, the Manhattan Project, of which was one of James Angleton's, Chief of the CIA's Counter-Intelligence Agencies pet projects, was also part of the UFO research and the "Fat Man" bomb constructed from technical studies taken from crashed space objects. (As listed by Wikipedia)

President Kennedy saw the crashed spacecraft and two alien bodies, and one was still alive and housed at the base. How would anyone know of this back in the day unless the President of the United States told them? Look at the photo of JFK at the Sandia Base! To date, this information has not been 'declassified'!

2. Documents confiscated by the LAPD, regarding Marilyn Monroe's telephone logs, were seized on behalf of the Attorney General and the Secret Service for safekeeping or destruction. However, Marilyn's friends have stated, on the record, that she did indeed call the President and the Attorney General numerous times until they changed their telephone number.

3. One week before Marilyn Monroe was assassinated, she said, at the CalNeva Lodge, that she was going to go public with the information she had on both Robert and John Kennedy. Besides, she told Jeanne Carmen on Thursday the 2nd that she was going to go public on Monday, August the 6th, 1962. Remember, Marilyn's phone, wiretapped, so everything she said was both listened to and recorded. Marilyn was injected - murdered on Saturday, August 4, 1962, at approximately 10:30 p.m.

4. Ironically, we now have the documentation that the CIA was working with the MOB, including Sam Giancana, *"...by placing botulism pills in his food..."* to poison Fidel Castro. However, Castro was too smart for the operatives; he had someone taste his food before he ate it – just one of the precautions Castro took. Also, the assets chickened out several times! (FBI memo dated **6/5/75 – attached, in part, B2b – 3 pages**)

5. The Red diary that Robert Kennedy was looking for the night she was killed was real. Marilyn wrote down what both RFK and JFK spoke about; call it pillow talk - so she could remember their conversations for the next time they met. After Marilyn was injected - murdered,

Robert and his bodyguards could not find the diary. Then on August 5, 1962, the Coroner's staff found it and locked it in the vault at the Coroner's office. The next day – it just *disappeared*. An LAPD OCID operative likely has a copy of the diary, and the content is real! In the journal, Marilyn said JFK told her he went to a secret base and saw the flying object. It was about 100 feet in length, dark glossy finish, appeared to be one piece, and could not see any doors, windows, exhausts, and it had a small wing on it. Also, they found two alien bodies, and one of the ET's was alive and still wearing a one-piece uniform – believe it or not...

Now, about this memo dated August 3, 1962, signed by James Angleton: Our agency sent an FOIA request to the CIA on July 11, 2017, with a copy of the memo. However, the memo we sent referenced ROCK DUST. We received an answer dated September 28, 2017 **(read it for yourself- attached - 7 pages, last page**); however, it had a reference of MOON DUST?

The CIA denies the authenticity of the memo, and in a letter dated April 10, 1995, Barry Harrelson, Senior Reviewer, CIA, *"...Those Agency officers who have reviewed the document consider it to be fraudulent..."* Then, who are "those Agency officers"? **Public law 80-253 was the National Security Act of 1947,** which in effect established the sweeping power of the intelligence community **to lie and deceive not only the Congress but the American people regarding the UFO invasion issue! (The MJ-12 Report, by Timothy Cooper, 6/13/99)**

This writer believes that the <u>*Central Intelligence Agency*</u> intentionally mislead the public; as a result of stating that the August 3, 1962 memo authored by CIA Counter-Intelligence Chief James Jesus Angleton was fraudulent. The language in the alleged fraudulent document includes **"inspect things from outer space"** which is equivalent to the **"UFO invasion issue"** wherein **Public law 80-253 was the National Security Act of 1947, allowing the CIA to lie, mislead or redact information of the same from the Congress and the American People. It looks like they did just that!**

CIA's Assassination Program

According to a video recording interview, William K. Harvey served as chief of ZR-RIFLE, "D" staff, and James Jesus Angleton reported to Harvey's "D" staff, the **CIA's assassination**

program in the early 1960s. Was Marilyn Monroe assassinated? After reviewing the official documents, video interviews, and our interview with LAPD OCID Ray Cadena – we say "YES."

Additionally, in a letter dated **August 17, 1962 - attached**, Robert Kennedy, Attorney General, stated in a memo, *"...According to National Security Action Memorandum 161, dated* ***June 9, 1962 – attached – 3 pages****, from the President, the Attorney General has been given primary responsibility for taking the initiative in the Government in ensuring the development of plans, programs, and action proposals to protect the internal security of the United States..."* **(See attached memo signed by Robert Kennedy, Attorney General**) So Robert had the authority to **'do whatever it takes'** to protect the internal security of the United States.

DOROTHY KILGALLEN

Dorothy Kilgallen died (was silenced - murdered?) on November 8, 1965 – a combination of barbiturates and alcohol – sound familiar? Dorothy knew she was a marked woman, so she gave copies of her notes to her friend and confidant, Florence Pritchett Smith. Just two days later, she died of the same causes – a combination of barbiturates and alcohol? Dorothy planned to blow the lid off of the JFK assassination.

In June 1966, Peter Lawford and his two children, along with Widow Jackie Kennedy spent two weeks together in Hawaii - **ATTACHED**. Dorothy Killgallen had information that may have linked Jackie to the assassination of her husband after her interview with Jack Rubenstein – who knows for sure? We will never know – Killgallen and Pritchett Smith were both killed just days apart.

There are several reasons to eliminate Marilyn Monroe. These are not good reasons unless you want to save the MOB's and the CIA's secret relationship. Or a political party's reputation, or to put it very simply, what we don't know about UFO's and what's at Area 51! And, the governments' upstanding ethical/moral standing before the American people is kept intact.

ATTACHMENTS

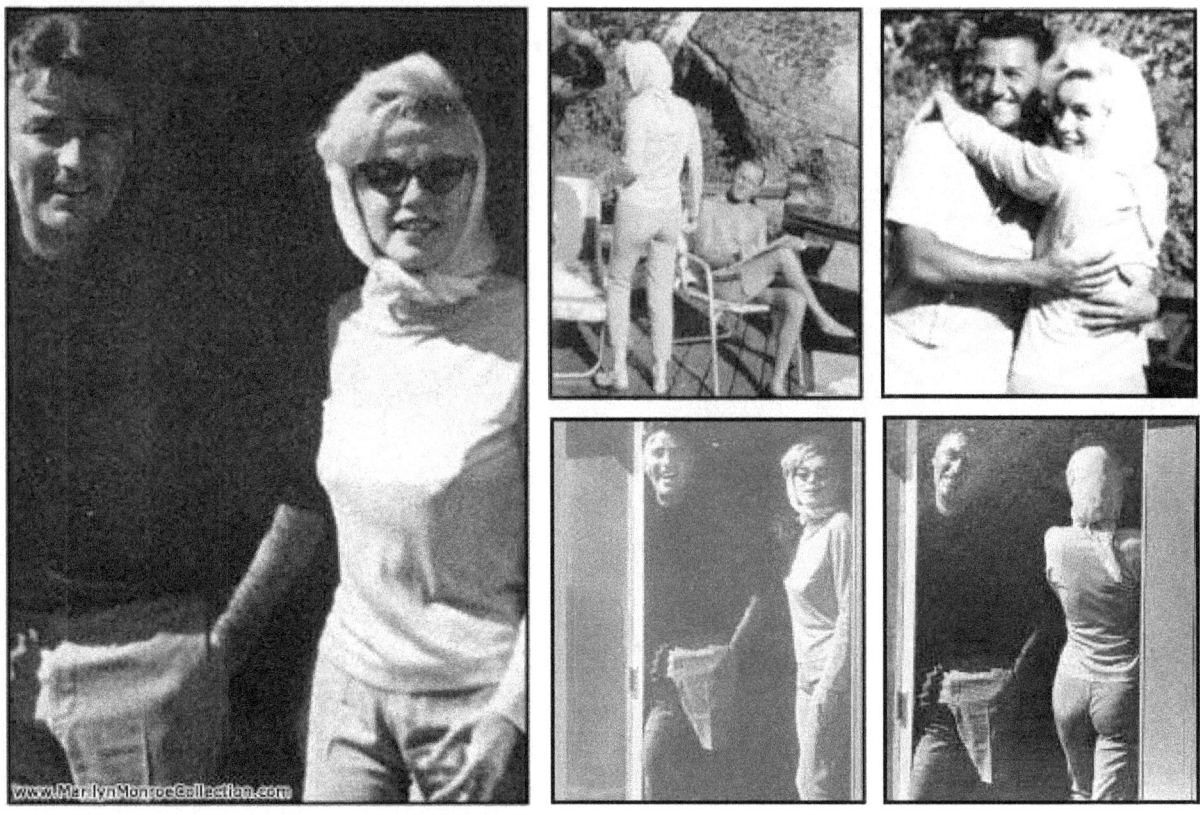

Marilyn at Cal-Neva Lodge the weekend of July 28 & 29, 1962, pictured with Buddy Greco, Frank Sinatra and Peter Lawford.

Giancana's reason for meeting Marilyn at the lodge was to convince her not to blow the whistle on the Kennedy's – in exchange, both John and Bobby Kennedy would back off of the prosecution of the Mob Boss.

NY 100-57673

DETAILS:

An article in the July 10, 1956, edition of the "Daily Worker" captioned "MILLERS Fly to England Friday" reflected that ARTHUR MILLER and actress MARILYN MONROE would fly to England on Friday (July 13, 1956) on a honeymoon and business trip.

The "Daily Worker" is an East Coast Communist daily newspaper.

b7c

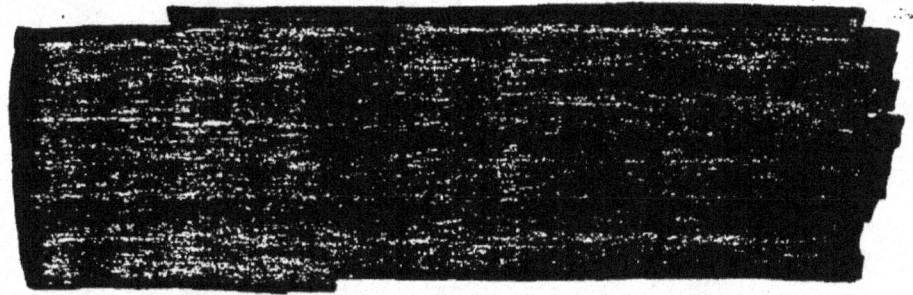

An article in the August 29, 1956, edition of the "New York Daily News" reflected that on that date, ARTHUR MILLER had arrived in New York from England to spend ten days to two weeks with his children. The article reflected that at the end of that time, MILLER would probably return to England to rejoin his bride, actress MARILYN MONROE.

b2  who has furnished reliable information in the past, on June 28, 1956, could furnish no information regarding the subject.

NY 100-57673

An article in the July 3, 1956 edition of the "Daily Worker" reflected that ARTHUR MILLER and MARILYN MONROE were married in a civil ceremony at White Plains, New York, on Friday, (June 29, 1956), and were subsequently remarried at Katonah, New York, on July 1, 1956, in the Jewish faith.

An article in the June 21, 1956, edition of the "New York Journal American", a daily newspaper, captioned "House To Quiz MILLER On Passport Dispute", reflected that ARTHUR MILLER, Broadway playwright, would interrupt his romance with Hollywood's MARILYN MONROE, "today" to appear before the House Committee on Un-American Activities (HCUA). According to the article, MILLER was scheduled to testify on his "passport battle" with the United States State Department and further that the members were certain to quiz MILLER on his alleged links with "some 29 organizations cited as Communist fronts by the House Committee on Un-American Activities or the United States Attorney General."

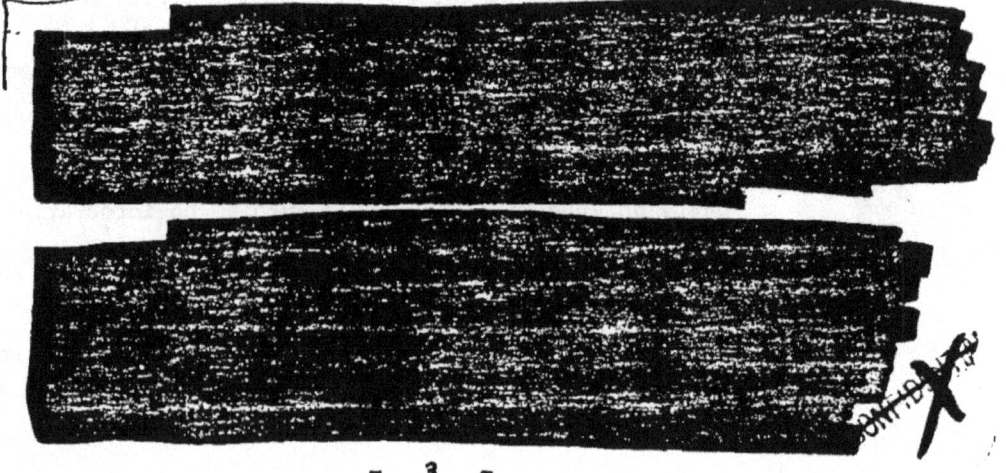

NY 100-57673

An article in the July 26, 1956, edition of the "New York Journal American" captioned "MILLER Prosecution Studied by BROWNELL" reflected that on July 25, 1956, the United States House of Representatives voted to cite MILLER for contempt of Congress and that the Justice Department was deciding whether to prosecute MILLER upon his return from England where he was honeymooning with actress MARILYN MONROE.

UNITED STATES GOVERNMENT

MEMORANDUM

TO: DIRECTOR, FBI DATE: 3/6/62

FROM: LEGAT, MEXICO (100-0)

SUBJECT: MARILYN MONROE
SM - C

The following information was received from [redacted] and [redacted] who have furnished reliable information in the past, on 2/28/62. Extreme care should be used in reporting any of this information to avoid disclosure of sources who were associating closely with subject during her visit to Mexico.

This source advised that MARILYN MONROE, the movie actress, was recently in Mexico on vacation and while in Mexico associated closely with certain members of the American Communist Group in Mexico (ACGM). Source characterized the ACGM as a loose association of a predominantly social nature of present and/or past members of the Communist Party, USA, and their friends and associates who share a common sympathy for Communism and the Soviet Union.

They advised that during the course of this visit a mutual infatuation arose between subject and FREDERICK VANDERBILT FIELD (Bufile 100-2278). This situation caused considerable dismay among Miss MONROE's entourage and also among the ACGM.

7 Bureau
(1 Liaison Section)
(2 New York)
(2 Los Angeles)
7 Mexico City (1 cc -
RSC:mms   1 cc - 100-1298 F. FIELD)
(14)   1 cc - 100-880 G. PEPPER)
                   1 cc - 100-1683 B. PRENSKY)
                   1 cc - 100-1488 D. PRENSKY)
                   1 cc - 105-649 ACGM)

105-40018-2

CONFIDENTIAL

MC 100-0

On 2/21/62, FIELD visited subject in her suite (#1110) at the Hotel Continental Hilton at 5:00 P.M. The visit was arranged through New York friends and was based on his former friendship with ARTHUR MILLER, her former husband. He stayed about an hour and she agreed to go with FIELD on 2/23/62 to Toluca, Mexico, for the day.

Subject arrived in Mexico on 2/19/62 from Miami. Her entry into Mexico reportedly was arranged by FRANK SINATRA through former President MIGUEL ALEMAN. She was accompanied by an agent, a hair dresser, and an interior decorator. The latter was identified as EUNICE CHURCHILL, a widow about 65 from Los Angeles. CHURCHILL said her husband was a violent trade unionist who was a functionary in the furniture workers section of the AF of L Carpenters Union who died four or five years ago. She identified him as a labor pioneer but did not identify him as a leftist. She is a part time interior decorator and also claims to be an assistant of Dr. WEXLEY, subject's analyst.

According to CHURCHILL, the subject was much disturbed by ARTHUR MILLER's marriage on 2/20/62 and feels like a "negated sex symbol." CHURCHILL said that subject "has a lot of leftist rubbed off from MILLER." Subject reportedly spent some time with ROBERT KENNEDY at the home of the PETER LAWFORDs in Hollywood. Subject reportedly challenged Mr. KENNEDY on some points proposed to her by MILLER.

Subject was acquainted with FIELD's background and principles and expressed curiosity as to his relationship with the VANDERBILT family.

On 2/24/62, subject traveled to Toluca, Mexico, to visit the native market. She was accompanied by FREDERICK VANDERBILT FIELD and _____ Later they returned to the FIELD home and were joined by BRYNA PRENSKY and her husband HENRY DAVID PRENSKY (Bufile 100-88237).

It became clear that a relationship was developing between subject and FIELD and considerable concern was expressed

- 2 -

CONFIDENTIAL

CONFIDENTIAL

MC 100-0

over this by various members of the ACGM, such as MAY BROOKS (Bufile 100-414864), CHARLES SMOLIKOFF (Bufile 100-12632), and RUTH CONDE, aka RUTH ASHMORE BROWN. CHARLES SMOLIKOFF said that FIELD was completely infatuated with MONROE. RUTH CONDE was very concerned for _____ who was excluded from a meeting of FIELD and subject on the night of 2/23/62.

On 2/25/62, EUNICE CHURCHILL said that Dr. WEXLEY did not like what was happening in the relationship between subject and FIELD and said that subject must get out with other people at once. She said subject is very vulnerable now because of her rejection by ARTHUR MILLER and also by JOE DiMAGGIO and FRANK SINATRA. She telephoned SINATRA to come and comfort her and he would not do it.

On the night of 2/24/62, she went with FIELD to a party at the home of EMILIO FERNANDEZ.

On 2/25/62, the subject had a date with GEORGE PEPPER (Bufile 100-254107) to view the movie "TORRERO" and go out with him afterwards; however, five minutes before he was to get her, she called and canceled the date and PEPPER was furious.

EUNICE CHURCHILL continued to express concern over subject's increasing dependence on FIELD.

On 2/27/62, subject attended a reception for Princess ANTONIO DE BRAGANZA, the infanta of Portugal. This was given at the home of DENNIS BOURKE and was attended by members of the staffs of various embassies and was completely nonpolitical in nature.

It is noted that _____ He advised that throughout the evening she expressed considerable curiosity about FIELD.

On 2/28/62, subject was to leave on a two-day trip to Taxco, Mexico, accompanied by FREDERICK VANDERBILT FIELD and his wife _____

CONFIDENTIAL

- 3 -

MC 100-0   CONFIDENTIAL   CONFIDENTIAL

RUTH CONDE said it was obvious that the subject was completely enamored with FIELD. She said that subject thinks FIELD is rich, stable, intellectual, and dependable. She said the situation is very hard on [redacted]. ⚹(K)

Mexico City newspapers reported subject left 3/2/62 en route to Los Angeles and San Francisco. ⚹U

Information copies of this communication are being directed to Los Angeles and New York as it contains information on activities of possible interest to those Divisions. ⚹U

CONFIDENTIAL

TOP SECRET

SUMMARY OF FACTS
INVESTIGATION OF CIA INVOLVEMENT IN PLANS TO
ASSASSINATE FOREIGN LEADERS

Table of Contents

		Page
A.	The Scope of the Investigation	
	1. Determining Jurisdiction	1
	2. Patrice Lumumba	3
	3. President Achmed Sukarno	4
	4. Concurrence of the President on Interpretation of Authority	4
B.	Participation of CIA Personnel in Plans to Attempt to Assassinate Fidel Castro	6
	1. Flying Cuban Exiles into Cuba	7
	2. 1960-61 and the Phase I Plans	8
	a. When the Plans Began	8
	b. The Development of the Phase I Plans According to the May 14, 1962 Memorandum to the Attorney General	10
	c. The Carrying Out of the Phase I Plan	13
	d. The Balletti Wiretap--Why the May 14, 1962 Memorandum was Prepared	15
	e. FBI Memoranda Concerning CIA Assassination Plans	19
	f. Additional Statements of Colonel Edwards re May 7, 1962 Briefing	23
	g. Statements of Colonel Edwards re Knowledge Inside CIA	24
	h. How the Plans Got Started	24
	i. Possible White House Direction or Approval of Plans	26
	(1) The Testimony of Richard Bissell	26
	(a) Eisenhower Administration	26
	(b) Kennedy Administration	26
	(2) The Testimony of Gordon Gray	29
	(3) The Testimony of Walt Rostow	29
	(4) The Interrogation of the Phase I Case Officer	29

DECLASSIFIED with portions redacted
JFK Assass. Rec. Collection Act of 1992
[redacted identifiers]
NARA date 5/24/00 By KSH

TOP SECRET

of the Attorney General of the United States following a complete oral briefing of him relevant to a sensitive CIA operation conducted during the period approximately August 1960 to May 1961." The oral briefing actually occurred in the offices of the Attorney General of the United States, Robert Kennedy, on May 7, 1962, and Attorney General Kennedy received a copy of the May 14, 1962 memorandum for the record. Attending the oral briefing were three people: Attorney General Kennedy, Sheffield Edwards and Lawrence Houston, General Counsel of the CIA.

    b. The Development of the Phase I Plans According to the May 14, 1962 Memorandum to the Attorney General

The May 14, 1962 memorandum was prepared by Sheffield Edwards and continued after the opening sentence: "In August 1960 the undersigned was approached by Mr. Richard Bissell, then Deputy Director for Plans of CIA, to explore the possibility of mounting this sensitive operation against Fidel Castro. It was thought that certain gambling interests, which had formerly been active in Cuba, might be willing and able to assist and further, might have both intelligence assets in Cuba and communication between Miami, Florida and Cuba."

The memorandum then related that an intermediary who was known to the CIA (Robert Maheu) was approached by Colonel

Sheffield Edwards "and asked to establish contact with a member or members of the gambling syndicate to explore their capabilities." The approach was to be made "...to the syndicate as appearing to represent big business organizations which wished to protect their interests in Cuba." The contact was made with a "syndicate" member who "showed interest in the possibility and indicated he had some contacts in Miami that he might use." The syndicate member supposedly told the CIA intermediary that the syndicate person "was not interested in any remuneration but would seek to establish capabilities in Cuba to perform the desired project."

The memorandum continued: "Towards the end of September 1960" contact with another syndicate member from Chicago, Sam Giancana, was made, and in turn an arrangement was made through Giancana for the CIA intermediary and his contact "to meet with a 'courier' who was going back and forth to Havana. From information received back by the courier the proposed operation appeared to be feasible and it was decided to obtain an official Agency approval in this regard. A figure of one hundred fifty thousand dollars was set by the Agency as a payment to be made on completion of the operation and to be paid only to the principal or principals who would conduct the operation in Cuba."

Central Intelligence Agency

Washington, D.C. 20505

28 September 2017

Rick Gentillalli, M.Ed.
Criminal Investigator

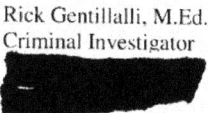

Dear Mr. Gentillalli:

This is a final response to your 24 May 2017 Freedom of Information Act (FOIA) request, received in the office of the Information and Privacy Coordinator on 11 July 2017, for **information or records on Dorothy Kilgallen and Howard Rothberg. [You] specifically request a memo dated 3 August 1962, signed by James Angleton, chief of CIA Counterintelligence, along with copies of the wiretaps (audio or transcripts) of telephone surveillance on the same two individuals and a clean copy of the memo related to the same subject matter.** We processed your request in accordance with the FOIA, 5 U.S.C. § 552, as amended, and the CIA Information Act, 50 U.S.C. § 3141, as amended.

We conducted a search for records on the same subject of your request and were unable to locate any responsive records. However, in response to your request and in an effort to assist you, our records located the enclosed document, consisting of eight pages, which includes a copy of the memo you enclosed in your request. Please be advised, however, that the memo dated 3 August 1962, included in the enclosed eight page document was determined to be fraudulent. Therefore, it was determined not to be a valid Agency document.

Although our searches were reasonably calculated to uncover all relevant documents, and it is highly unlikely that repeating those searches would change the result, you nevertheless have the legal right to appeal the finding of no records responsive to your request. As the CIA Information and Privacy Coordinator, I am the CIA official responsible for this determination. You have the right to appeal this response to the Agency Release Panel, in my care, within 90 days from the date of this letter. Please include the basis of your appeal.

If you have any questions regarding our response, you may contact us at:

Central Intelligence Agency
Washington, DC 20505
Information and Privacy Coordinator
703-613-3007 (Fax)

Please be advised that you may seek dispute resolution services from the CIA's FOIA Public Liaison or from the Office of Government Information Services (OGIS) of the National Archives and Records Administration. OGIS offers mediation services to help resolve disputes between FOIA requesters and Federal agencies. You may reach CIA's FOIA Public Liaison at:

703-613-1287 (FOIA Hotline)

The contact information for OGIS is:

Office of Government Information Services
National Archives and Records Administration
8601 Adelphi Road – OGIS
College Park, MD 20740-6001
202-741-5770
877-864-6448
202-741-5769 (fax)
ogis@nara.gov

Contacting the CIA's FOIA Public Liaison or OGIS does not affect your right to pursue an administrative appeal.

Sincerely,

Allison Fong
Information and Privacy Coordinator

Enclosure

C00566845

file copy

ROUTING AND RECORD SHEET

SUBJECT: (Optional) Coordination: JFK Assassination Document (FBI referral)

FROM: Barry Harrelson, Reviewer
CSI/HRG
402 Ames

EXTENSION: 30171

DATE: 3-25-93

TO: (Officer designation, room number, and building)	DATE RECEIVED	DATE FORWARDED	OFFICIAL'S INITIALS	COMMENTS
1. DCI/FIO 7E12 OHB	3/29/93		Ul	Becky, For your review, FBI memorandum dated 12/23/63 (Brennan to Sullivan) containing CIA information. We are proposing "Release-in-Full" for this document. [03]
2.				
3.				
4. Barry Harrelson CSI/HRG				
5. 402 Ames				
6.				
7.				
8.				
9.				No objection to full release of this document. [03]
10.				
11.				
12.				
13.				
14.				
15.				

CIA SPECIAL COLLECTIONS
RELEASE AS SANITIZED

Declassified and Approved for Release
by the Central Intelligence Agency
Date: 7/14/03

JFK ACT RELEASE

FORM 610 USE PREVIOUS EDITIONS
1-92

UNITED STATES GOVERNMENT

Memorandum

TO : Mr. W. C. Sullivan DATE: 12/23/63

FROM : Mr. D. J. Brennan, Jr.

SUBJECT: RELATIONS WITH CENTRAL INTELLIGENCE AGENCY (CIA) Lee Oswald

Reference is made to memorandum dated 12/19/63, from Mr. Brennan to Mr. Sullivan. Pursuant to instructions, Agent Papich met with John McCone, Director, CIA, on 12/23/63, to confront the CIA Director with false statements attributed to him by Mr. DeLoach's sources. The Liaison Agent is reporting this meeting in some detail so that you may have full appreciation of all aspects.

Agent Papich advised McCone that he had a piece of business which needed ironing out before the end of the year. The Agent explained that since the assassination of President Kennedy, there have been various types of stories circulated concerning the case and the evidence collected; that some of these stories could immediately be discounted; and that there was certain information received by the Bureau which very directly affected relations between the Bureau and CIA. The Agent stated that certain information had reached such proportion to be most alarming and that the Agent had requested permission from Mr. Hoover to discuss the matter with the CIA Director.

McCone was then told that he was charged with being the source of information conveyed to a high Government official and to Drew Pearson in that he, McCone, had stated that CIA had uncovered a plot in Mexico City indicating that Lee Harvey Oswald had received $6,500 to assassinate President Kennedy. The Agent elaborated by stating that if this were true, McCone had endeavored to leave the impression with certain people that CIA had developed information not known to the Bureau and, in essence, made the Bureau look ridiculous. The Agent advised that if McCone had made such statements, we could only assume that he was employing vicious and underhanded tactics since he and officials of his agency fully well knew that the story concerning the $6,500 had been proved to be absolutely false. McCone's attention was directed to the Alvarado interrogation, Alvarado's admission that he had fabricated the information and the subsequent

1 - Mr. Belmont
1 - Mr. DeLoach
1 - Mr. Sullivan
1 - Mr. Branigan
1 - Liaison
1 - Mr. Papich
JP:chs
(7)

NOT RECORDED
199 JAN 2 1964

22 DEC 31 1963

Memo Mr. Brennan to Mr. Sullivan
Re: RELATIONS WITH CIA

corroboration of the polygraph. (S)

McCone was very visibly incensed and left the impression that he might at any moment ask the Agent to leave. After pausing a few moments, he made the following statements: (S)

(1) He stated that he has never talked to Drew Pearson in his life; that he has never sent any kind of message to Pearson directly or indirectly and that he does not have any intention of communicating with Pearson. He briefly referred to the fact that he has been the target of attacks by Pearson, one of these occurring within the last two weeks. (S)

(2) With regard to the "$6,500 story," McCone advised that as soon as the original report was received from his people in Mexico City, he contacted President Johnson and informed him of the development. He explained to the President that this was a matter which required intensive interrogation of Alvarado and that CIA had coordinated very closely with the FBI. He told the President that Alvarado would be kept in a safe house by CIA until the FBI was satisfied that all necessary investigative action had taken place. (S)

(3) McCone advised that he has not been critical of the Bureau; that if he had any criticism he would confer directly with the Bureau and not get involved in malicious gossip. He commented that in connection with the Oswald case, he has encountered people who have been critical of the Bureau and the Secret Service and he, McCone, has gone to the defense of both agencies. (S)

(S) McCone was left in an angry mood but he did retain his composure throughout. Before the Agent left, McCone inquired about the status of FBI - CIA relations in general and the Agent replied that they were satisfactory. He also asked about the Director's health to which the Agent answered that the Director was in excellent health.

As indicated above, no statement was made which in any way might jeopardize the security of Mr. DeLoach's sources.

ACTION:

For information.

FOR OFFICIAL USE ONLY

CIA S... ONS
RE...
2000   10 April 1995

MEMORANDUM FOR: Mr. Grant P. Harmon
                  Unit Chief, JFK Taskforce
                  Federal Bureau of Investigation

FROM: Barry Harrelson, Senior Reviewer
                  Historical Review Group
                  Center for the Study of Intelligence
                  Central Intelligence Agency

SUBJECT: Authenticity of Document

   1. This is in response to your request to this office to review the attached document and advise if it is a valid Agency document or something made up using an Agency reports format and information either entirely made up or from other sources. The 3 August 1962 document purports to tie Dorothy Kilgallen, Marilyn Monroe and former Attorney General, Robert Kennedy, together with knowledge of an number of matters, including the plot to kill Castro.

   2. Those Agency officers who have reviewed the document consider it to be fradulent. While the format resembles a "reports" form used in the 1960's, the substantive information and presentation is foreign to normal presentaion or collection efforts. Also, the control stamps and other administrative items are not typical of CIA reports written during the 1960's.

   3. If you have any further questions in this regard, please call me directly at (703) 351-2909.

                                     Barry Harrelson

BH:gb

FOR OFFICIAL USE ONLY

Real or Fraudulent

CENTRAL INTELLIGENCE AGENCY

NOT FOR PUBLICATI

COUNTRY: New York, US
SUBJECT: Marilyn Monroe
REPORT NO. ■■■■
DATE DIST: 3 August 1962
NO PAGES: ■■
REFERENCES: MOON DUST Project ■

3 August 1962

Wiretap of telephone conversation between reporter Dorothy Kilgallen and her close friend, Howard Rothberg (A); from wiretap of telephone conversation of Marilyn Monroe and Attorney General Robert Kennedy (B). Appraisal of Content:

1. Rothberg discussed the apparent ■■■■■■ of subject with Kilgallen and the break up with the Kennedys. Rothberg told Kilgallen that she was attending Hollywood parties hosted by the "inner circle" among Hollywood's elite and was becoming the talk of the town again. Rothberg indicated in so many words, that she had secrets to tell, no doubt arising from her trists with the President and the Attorney General. One such "secret" mentions the visit by the President at a secret air base for ■■■ purposes of inspecting things from outer space. Kilgallen replied that she knew what might be the source of visit. In the mid-fifties Kilgallen learned of secret effort by US and UK governments to identify the origins of crashed spacecraft and dead bodies, from a British government official. Kilgallen believed the story may have come from the New ■■■■■■■■■ in the late forties. Kilgallen said that if the story is true, it would cause terrible embarrass■■■ Jack and his plans to have NASA put men on the moon.

2. Subject repeatedly called the Attorney General and complained about the way she was being ignored by the President and his brother.

3. Subject threatened to hold a press conference and would tell all.

4. Subject made reference to "bases" in Cuba and knew of the President's plan to kill Castro.

5. Subject made reference to her "diary of secrets" and what the newspapers would do with such disclosures.

Office of the Attorney General
Washington, D.C.

August 17, 1962

MEMORANDUM TO HEADS OF DEPARTMENTS AND AGENCIES:

Pursuant to National Security Action Memorandum 161, dated June 9, 1962 from the President, The Attorney General has been given primary responsibility for taking the initiative in the Government in ensuring the development of plans, programs, and action proposals to protect the internal security of the United States. His office has also been given supervision of the two interdepartmental committees concerned with internal security--the Interdepartmental Intelligence Conference (IIC) and the Interdepartmental Committee on Internal Security (ICIS)--which have been under the supervision of the National Security Council.

There is certainly a continuing need for the IIC and ICIS. The functions and responsibilities of these two interdepartmental committees will be as defined in their charters issued by the NSC on July 18, 1949 (amended September 10, 1954; see NSC 5425/1) and approved by the President. I would like their organizations and procedures to continue unchanged, except that their reports or recommendations heretofore directed to the National Security Council will now be directed to me as Attorney General. It is anticipated that problems and proposals under consideration in the committees will continue to require the scheduling of meetings and the time of departmental staffs, as has been the case in the past.

I trust that all departments and agencies will continue to cooperate with the chairmen of the two committees as they have in the past to assure the competent and expeditious handling of the committees' business.

Attorney General

THE WHITE HOUSE
WASHINGTON

CONFIDENTIAL

NSC REFERRAL NOT REQUIRED

June 9, 1962

NATIONAL SECURITY ACTION MEMORANDUM 161

TO:
The Secretary of State
The Secretary of Defense
The Secretary of the Treasury
The Secretary of Commerce
The Attorney General
The Director of Central Intelligence
Military Representative of the President
Administrator, Federal Aviation Agency
Chairman, Atomic Energy Commission

SUBJECT: U. S. Internal Security Programs

1. In line with my continuing effort to give primary responsibility for the initiative on major matters of policy and administration in a given field to a key member of my Administration, I will look to the Attorney General to take the initiative in the government in ensuring the development of plans, programs, and action proposals to protect the internal security of the United States. I will expect him to prepare recommendations, in collaboration with other departments and agencies in the government having the responsibility for internal security programs, with respect to those matters requiring Presidential action.

CONFIDENTIAL

(EXECUTIVE REGISTRY FILE_____)
(   )

THE WHITE HOUSE
WASHINGTON

CONFIDENTIAL   - 2 -

2. Accordingly, I have directed that the two interdepartmental committees concerned with internal security--the Interdepartmental Intelligence Conference (IIC) and the Interdepartmental Committee on Internal Security (ICIS)--which have been under the supervision of the National Security Council, will be transferred to the supervision of the Attorney General. The continuing need for these committees and their relationship to the Attorney General will be matters for the Attorney General to determine.

cc: J. Edgar Hoover, Chairman Interdepartmental Intelligence Conference
John F. Doherty, Chairman Interdepartmental Committee on Internal Security
A. Russell Ash, NSC Staff

CONFIDENTIAL

CONFIDENTIAL

CENTRAL INTELLIGENCE AGENCY

EXECUTIVE MEMORANDUM

NSC REFERRAL NOT REQUIRED

OFFICE OF THE DIRECTOR

EXECUTIVE MEMORANDUM No. 8

DATE 13 June 1962

MEMORANDUM FOR:

DEPUTY DIRECTOR (PLANS)
DEPUTY DIRECTOR (INTELLIGENCE)
DEPUTY DIRECTOR (RESEARCH)
DEPUTY DIRECTOR (SUPPORT)
COMPTROLLER
INSPECTOR GENERAL
GENERAL COUNSEL
ASSISTANT DIRECTOR
   FOR NATIONAL ESTIMATES

Director of Security

DD/P - Attn: Chief, CI

O/Exec.Dir./jrc
Distribution:
1 - each addressee
1 - Exec. Dir.
1 - ER - w/basic

This memorandum contains information for the addressee. Addressees may give this memorandum additional circulation among their components as required. All copies should be destroyed or filed, upon completion of circulation. A master file will be kept in the Executive Director's Office and will be available upon request.

CONFIDENTIAL

Sandia Laboratory

June 1966, Peter Lawford and his two children, along with Widow Jackie Kennedy, spent two weeks together in Hawaii.

CHAPTER 6

The Players Involved

We mentioned the **HARDCOPY – 1992 Investigation into the death of MARILYN MONROE 3/4 (YouTube)** and what **Dan Stewart** told them – the infamous "Ray" –

Dan Stewart's LAPD partner was William C. Jordan, another LAPD OCID Detective Lieutenant. A little bit about Bill, after he retired from LAPD, he opened up WCJ INC. Private Investigations located in Westlake Village, CA 91359-4647. His background is typical of many OCID operatives, and Bill fits right in. Mr. Jordan enlisted in the US Marine Corp in 1941 at the age of fifteen. After serving three years in the Pacific area as a combat Marine, he received and honorably discharged on November 18, 1945. Mr. Jordan holds a Bachelor of Science degree from Los Angeles State College, as well as a Master's of Science degree from the University of Southern California.

After spending two years on the Beverly Hills Police Department, **Bill Jordan** joined LAPD graduating as the number one Honor Graduate in his class in May of 1954. While at the Intelligence Division, he was assigned to numerous personal protection assignments: Madam Nu and her daughter from Viet Nam, Hubert Humphrey, Jack Kennedy, Martin Luther King, and Lyndon Johnson, to name a few. Mr. Jordan also offered the District Attorney's office any help they wanted relating to the 1982 Marilyn Monroe re-investigation in a letter dated **October 1, 1982** - attached.

In 1962, both Dan and Bill were called out to go to Marilyn's house the morning after she died and make an OCID report.

More importantly, they were both also part of the LAPD's "Special Unit Senator" (SUS); the unit comprised of many OCID officers to investigate the assassination of Robert Kennedy.

The RFK LAPD Microfilm, Volume 75 - attached, as preserved by the Mary Ferrell Foundation, included the SUS final report, and it states that on **June 5, 1968, page 253**, 8:30 a.m. "…Intelligence Division Sergeants **George Arnold and Ray Cadena** were dispatched to the hospital at the direction of the Chief's Office. Their assignment was to evaluate the security measures and report their findings directly to **Chief Reddin**. Additionally, both were instructed to make necessary changes as they deemed necessary and to remain there as additional security..."

At approximately 1:44 a.m. on June 6, 1968, Senator Robert F. Kennedy expired. **On page 255 of the same report, from 3:00 a.m. to 9:15 a.m.** "...Sergeant **William Jordan** and Officer **Dan Stewart** were assigned to attend the autopsy of Senator Kennedy..." The report continues, and you can read the entirety of it at your leisure - attached. Hmmm...why would LAPD OCID be the elite agency to oversee the autopsy of Senator Robert Kennedy - shows just how powerful OCID was.

This is where LAPD OCID Officer Dan Stewart mentioned the name "Ray" in the **HARDCOPY – 1992 Investigation into the death of MARILYN MONROE 3/4 (YouTube.)** As you can see, Ray Cadena and George Arnold were the two OCID officers watching Marilyn Monroe's house and picked up Robert Kennedy at the Santa Monica Airport on the afternoon of August 4, 1962. You will also see that Ray and George are the two who participated in the Marilyn Monroe Murder. Both LAPD OCID Officers Ray and George were also CIA assets and did individual assignments for the CIA. We believe that the Marilyn Monroe Murder was one of these assignments.

INTERVIEW OF RAY CHARLES CADENA, RET LAPD OCID – 11-14-16
Ray Charles Cadena DOB 10/21/19**; Santee, CA 92071 (619) 990-****

R. C. CADENA: hello

INV. GENTILLALLI: hi, uh, are you Ray

R. C. CADENA: I'm Ray

INV. GENTILLALLI: yah, Ray my name is Rick, I'm an investigator

R. C. CADENA: yah

INV. GENTILLALLI: um, hopefully, I have the right person; uh, I'm trying to find a Ray Cadena, Ray Charles Cadena who worked for LAPD, with a, with Dan Stewart, and I think Marvin

R. C. CADENA: who are you?

INV. GENTILLALLI: pardon me

R. C. CADENA: who are you?

INV. GENTILLALLI: my name is Rick Gentillalli

R. C. CADENA: you said that

INV. GENTILLALLI: and I have a card, I can give that to you if you like, I'm, I'm conducting ah, well we're working on the Marilyn Monroe case

R. C. CADENA: you're working on the what?

INV. GENTILLALLI: the Marilyn Monroe case

R. C. CADENA: I can't hear you

INV. GENTILLALLI: I'm sorry, we're working on the Marilyn Monroe case, and I'll give you a card

R. C. CADENA: on which case, the Marilyn Monroe?

INV. GENTILLALLI: yea

R. C. CADENA: you got to be kidding me!

INV. GENTILLALLI: no sir, we're not here to get anyone involved, the only thing to do is hopefully do a movie, and we want everything to be accurate because everything that is out there is inaccurate, everything, uh we've already tried

R. C. CADENA: you don't want the true stuff coming out, and people all over this country do not want it, the true stuff coming out

INV. GENTILLALLI: well, the people we spoke with, well we got, I know this sounds weird we got kind of authorization from Washington through a person we are working with, his name is **** ****, he's former, let's say the department of defense operative, and we got…

R. C. CADENA: you got the right, Ray Cadena, I was in work there, I worked intelligence division for 12 years, and I don't want to have a thing to do with you

INV. GENTILLALLI: really

R. C. CADENA: because I don't want to have anything to do with you, I don't have to explain myself

INV. GENTILLALLI: no I understand that sir, we're not here to uh

R. C. CADENA: and that's when you leave, I don't wish you well, you're into an area that should be left alone, that's all I'll say

INV. ATENCIO: it's that, that fine of a line?

INV. GENTILLALLI: no one has told us that, we spoke with Dan Stewart, he's still alive, we spoke with a person who heard the tapes

INV. ATENCIO: in palm springs

INV. GENTILLALLI: in Palm Springs, at Dan Stewarts house

R. C. CADENA: how did you find me?

INV. GENTILLALLI: well it wasn't easy; we have a list of all of the ocid officers

R. C. CADENA: all who?

INV. GENTILLALLI: the OCID officers, ok there are two different lists, there's the old list, the original, and then there are the newer officers who came on board, I have both of the lists; I'll be very honest how we found you, I should say, Dan Stewart, years ago did an interview, and he was explaining how he used to be a bodyguard, and he used to guard, Robert Kennedy and John Kennedy when they would have their flings, at different motels in Los Angeles, hotels I should say… he said when he worked the Kennedy, Dan Stewart worked the Robert Kennedy shooting, and when he went to the hospital, he would finally go there, when Kennedy was shot, he said there were already two ocid officers there, he said one of them was you, so that's how your name came up, and it wasn't, I'm a good investigator, I'm retired from the federal government, and it wasn't easy finding you, I can tell you that, it's not like someone is going to find you and I'm not going to disclose any information about you to anyone.

R. C. CADENA: mumbling about his dog
6:49 p.m.

INV. ATENCIO: what kind is he?

R. C. CADENA: huh

INV. ATENCIO what kind is he?

R. C. CADENA: golden retriever

INV. ATENCIO: they're sweet

R. C. CADENA: there are a hundred pounds of him

INV. ATENCIO: he's sweet, a family dog

R. C. CADENA: you probably have Sor Dorum on there, on your list, scratch him, he died three months ago

INV. ATENCIO: aww

INV. GENTILLALLI: oh he did

R. C. CADENA: yea, most of us from that era are dead; I just came out of rehab, a center

INV. ATENCIO: well you look great for coming out of that, I mean you look great in general I don't even know your age but

R. C. CADENA: 88

INV. ATENCIO: I see

INV. GENTILLALLI: you look very good for 88, you did well

INV. ATENCIO: yeah

R. C. CADENA: I don't want to get involved in this at all!

INV. GENTILLALLI: ok, I do understand that um

R. C. CADENA: ...we did a good job, it's something that had to be done, and we did it!

INV. GENTILLALLI: right

INV. GENTILLALLI: well let me go one step further, I have, I found a document, ok this is a document from John Kennedy when he was president, he gave his brother, Robert Kennedy authority to, they took over the FBI position, I forget the name of the agency but he gave this to Robert Kennedy, the attorney general, authority for internal security of the united states, now that means that Robert Kennedy could have told anyone to do what he told them to do ...exterminated somebody because he had the authority to do it and there's no repercussion to anyone, I have that document, I just got it from the CIA

R. C. CADENA: I wish you well, but I'm not going to get involved. And uh, my friend George Carr (note: he uses the last name Carr instead of Arnold) is a housebound

INV. GENTILLALLI: George Carr

R. C. CADENA: George Carr, he's housebound

INV. ATENCIO: which means?

R. C. CADENA: he can't talk ...he still has his mental faculties, but he can't talk loud enough so you can hear him, he has severe emphysema

INV. GENTILLALLI: aww, that's terrible

R. C. CADENA: thank you very much, good luck

INV. GENTILLALLI: can I ask you one question, you don't have to answer it...the two officers who were there, possibly you, I'm not saying you, and then the other officer, I believe was Marvin

R. C. CADENA: was what?

INV. GENTILLALLI: Marvin Innone, but I don't know, that's what I'm trying to figure out who the other officer…

R. C. CADENA: Marvin Innone was the chief in "…", I think he's dead

INV. GENTILLALLI: he is still alive

R. C. CADENA: is he?

INV. GENTILLALLI: yah he's alive, and I do know the two officers picked-up Kennedy at Santa Monica airport, I know who the pilot is, Hal Connors, it's called desert commuter airlines

INV. ATENCIO: there's a lot of time searching

INV. GENTILLALLI: nobody knows what we know

INV. ATENCIO: and we don't tell anybody, at this point

INV. GENTILLALLI: so this is what I am trying to find out, and that is … the other, the whole thing, the officer, I know Fred Otash went there, later on, to clean everything up, I know that because of the person we interviewed, Clemmons actually, Otash and Clemmons crossed paths when Clemmons arrived

INV. ATENCIO: that's what we gathered so far, we're trying to put the puzzle together, you know

INV. GENTILLALLI: I don't know who the other officer was

R. C. CADENA: you are going to write a book?

INV. GENTILLALLI: well ultimately

INV. ATENCIO: my life, I can relate a lot of my life to hers, as myself growing up, and so I have this connection personally with my past and so on, this passion, you know… childhood and so on, We just want to kind of find out

R. C. CADENA: are you married

INV. GENTILLALLI: good friends

R. C. CADENA: no, I don't want to get involved in all that, the people I know who do know something about it, aren't going to talk to you

INV. GENTILLALLI: right, well I'll go one step further, there's one person, who has copies of the file, and a transcript of the tape

INV. ATENCIO: he's still alive, he used to work for the OCID, and has copies of the, all the documents

INV. GENTILLALLI: he has the entire ocid file

INV. ATENCIO: the Kennedy's and of Marilyn, so…

INV. GENTILLALLI: we're in contact with him

R. C. CADENA: I've read all of the files

INV. GENTILLALLI: I'm sure you were one of the authors for some of them, um, I don't mean this jokingly, I have a 100% respect for you

R. C. CADENA: thank you, but my wife is going in for chemotherapy tomorrow

INV. ATENCIO: aww

R. C. CADENA: and ah, I have to …

INV. GENTILLALLI: ok sir

R. C. CADENA: so goodnight

INV. ATENCIO: well thank you for your time

R. C. CADENA: certainly

INV. GENTILLALLI: I did give you my card, I know it's totally up to you, but if for some reason you wanted to call or…

INV. ATENCIO: or anything

INV. GENTILLALLI: anything at all

R. C. CADENA: ok

INV. ATENCIO: we come from Hemet, and next we're going to Santa Monica, to attempt to try to talk to Marvin

INV. GENTILLALLI: Marvin

INV. GENTILLALLI: Innone

R. C. CADENA: who?

INV. GENTILLALLI: Marvin Innone

INV. ATENCIO: Marvin if he's still alive, we feel that we're finding the need

R. C. CADENA: he retired as deputy chief of Los Angeles

INV. GENTILLALLI: no he, he retired as chief of Beverly hills

R. C. CADENA: no he didn't retire as chief of Beverly Hills, he retired to be the chief of Beverly Hills, but Beverly Hills was a separate department

INV. GENTILLALLI: oh, ok, ok

INV. ATENCIO: I appreciate your clarification, it's not easy putting this together, we appreciate, where, who belongs to which department

INV. GENTILLALLI: nothing will be disclosed about you

R. C. CADENA: good by!

INV. GENTILLALLI: alright sir

INV. ATENCIO: thank you for your time, and happy New Year, and good luck with everything

INV. GENTILLALLI: thank you, sir,

INV. ATENCIO: alright, good night, I'll lock this door…ok, thank you

INV. GENTILLALLI: thank you, sir

R.C. CADENA: I'm going – closed the door on us!

INTERVIEW CONCLUDED

The interview technics used may be confusing to the public; however, sometimes, you have to lead the interviewee in a direction where you don't ask the correct question to solicit information unbeknownst to the subject. In the next few chapters, this will come together, and a detailed chronology presented surrounding the Murder of Marilyn Monroe!

ATTACHMENTS

WCJ INC.

Investigative Consultants   Los Angeles   New York   London   Paris   Geneva

Post Office Box 4993
Westlake Village, California 91359

(213) 457-1038

October 1, 1982

Michael Carrol
Assistant District Attorney
District Attorney's Office
210 W. Temple Street
Los Angeles, CA 90012

Dear Mike:

Just wanted to drop you a note to thank you for your time in talking to the British BBC representative, Tony Summers. I, for one, certainly realize that it is not feasible to discuss open cases with strangers, certainly members of the press. I tried to explain to Tony that even though off-the-record in England apparently still ethically means off-the-record, but because of numerous problems in the states that didn't carry too much weight over here and not to take it personally.

As a former detective lieutenant with the Los Angeles Police Department and having worked with your office on numerous cases, I certainly understand the difficulty. I do deeply appreciate your courtesy in giving Tony what information you could. Thanks again for your kindness. Hope to see you in the near future.

Sincerely,

William C. Jordan

WCJ/sp

MARY FERRELL FOUNDATION
preserving the legacy

HOME   STARTING POINTS   ARCHIVE   RESOURCES   HELP   ABOUT US   ADV SEARCH   RIF SEARCH

home / archive / documents / rfk assassination documents / special unit senator lapd collection /

RFK LAPD Microfilm, Volume 75 (SUS Final Report)

PDF version
32790K

Table of Contents   **Document View**

Search Document »

+ 55		Investigation Summary of the Senator Robert F. Kennedy Assassination (continued)
+ 55		II. Summary of the Investigation (continued)
+ 55		The Assassin (continued)
+ 61		Investigations of Possible Conspiracies
+ 96		Case Preparation for Trial
+ 106		Legal Processes
+ 109		Related Events Since the Assassination
+ 117		Conclusions
+ --		Volume II
+ --		III. Assassination
+ --		Kennedy's Plans and Activities
+ 119		Kennedy's Activities from June 2nd to June 4h
+ 122		The Ambassador Hotel
+ 123		Security
+ 124		Security Provided by Los Angeles Police Department
+ 127		Example of Kennedy Party Attitude Toward the Police Department
+ 131		Personal Security
+ 133		Security Provided by The Ambassador Hotel
+ 136		Election Night at the Hotel
+ 140		Press Coverage at The Ambassador
+ 143		Victory Speech
+ 146		From The Stage to The Kitchen
+ 149		The Shooting
+ 155		Sirhan's Capture
+ 162		Victims and Witnesses in Kitchen
+ --		Medical Treatment and Autopsy (Senator Kennedy)
+ 177		Other Victims of the Shooting
+ 185		Police Participation
+ 186		The Ambassador Hotel
+ 227		Central Receiving Hospital
+ 238		Good Samaritan Hospital
+ 264		Functions of Rampart Patrol and Detectives
+ 280		Emergency Control Center and Security at Parker Center
+ 296		Transfer of Senator Kennedy's Body from Good Samaritan Hospital to he Los Angeles Int'l. Airport
+ --		IV. The Assassin
+ --		Volume III
+ 299		Sirhan's Activities the Night of June 4, 1968
+ 305		Sirhan's Arrest and Arraignment
+ --		Identification of Sirhan
+ 315		Gun Provided Link to Sirhan
+ 317		Adel Sirhan at the Pasadena Police Department
+ 318		Follow-Up at Pasadena
+ 329		Sirhan's Vehicle
+ --		Sirhan's Background (Profile Analysis)
+ 338		Early Years in Jerusalem
+ 344		Chronicle of Sirhan's Family in The United States
+ 353		School History in United States
+ 361		Employment History
+ 370		Financial Status
+ 374		Medical History
+ 379		Criminal History
+ 381		Social Activities
+ 389		Religious Background

Pages 253 255 2

POLICE PARTICIPATION

5:55 a.m.

Black Panther spokesman Wilber Terry and three of his followers left the area in a blue station wagon.

6:20 a.m.

The crowd outside had dwindled to approximately fifteen persons; no militants were in the group.

6:20 a.m.

Surgery performed on Senator Kennedy was terminated. A short time later he was returned to the Intensive Care Ward. The route taken from the ninth floor was the reverse of that taken earlier from the fifth floor to surgery. Sgt. Swinart was in charge providing security during this transfer. Lt. Tackaberry assigned Officer Stolle to escort the Senator from the ninth floor.

6:25 a.m.

Dr. Paul T. Wertlake, a pathologist, gave Sgt. D. D. Varney a glass vial containing bullet fragments which had been removed from the mastoid area of the Senator's head. Varney transported this item to Rampart Station where it was booked as evidence. Before the vial left the hospital, the items were photographed by Mr. L. R. Gaines, Scientific Investigation Division.

7:00 a.m.

Sergeant Varney returned to the hospital and received a second vial from Lt. Hogue. This vial containing a bullet fragment had been given to Hogue by Dr. Wertlake moments earlier. Sergeant Varney took this vial to Rampart Station.

-251-

7:30 a.m.

Secret Service Agent Darwin Horn met with Inspector Sporrer. Horn informed him that the Secret Service had been assigned to provide personal security for the Senator and his family. The Secret Service, however, was not assuming the responsibility for the investigation of the crime. They then conferred with Margaret Wherry, a hospital administrator, and made arrangements for screening employees.

Margaret Wherry later met with the press to offer them the use of the hospital's auditorium located a half block northeast of the hospital on Lucas Street. Some press members rejected her offer demanding that they be allowed inside the hospital. After discussing this problem with Sporrer and Horn, she allowed the press inside. She provided a room equipped with telephones on the main floor.

This created an additional security problem, and extra officers were positioned at key locations to prevent infiltration into restricted areas. Ultimate decisions to permit entry into restricted areas were left to Inspector Sporrer.

8:00 a.m.

Thirty-one officers and three sergeants from Metropolitan Division day watch relieved all of the officers on duty at the hospital. Sgt. M. Yturralde assumed charge of inside security with fifteen officers. The remaining sixteen officers, under Sgt. B. J. Remas, remained outside the hospital to provide exterior security. Metropolitan Division was mobilized into twelve-hour shifts and assigned to provide all the security at the hospital.

Captain W. T. Smith relieved Captain Fudge and assumed the duty as senior officer-in-charge. Inspector Sporrer had gone to Parker Center to give the exposed photographs of Senator Kennedy to Chief Reddin.

8:30 a.m.

Intelligence Division Sergeants G. O. Arnold and R. C. Cadena were dispatched to the hospital at the direction of the Chief's Office. Their assignment was to evaluate the security measures and report their findings directly to Chief Reddin. Additionally, both were instructed to make necessary changes as they deemed necessary and to remain there as additional security.

9:00 a.m.

Lieutenant B. E. Sanderson, Rampart Day Watch Commander, assumed the duty of senior officer-in-charge. Captain Smith resumed his normal assignment as Commander of Business Office Division.

10:00 a.m.

Sergeant R. F. McGuire and Officer C. H. Wilson were dispatched to the International Airport to transport the other Kennedy children to the Good Samaritan Hospital.

3:00 p.m.

Sergeants K. M. Cleary and G. R. Souza, Intelligence Division, were sent to the International Airport to provide security and transportation for Mrs. Martin L. King. They drove her to the Good Samaritan Hospital, arriving at 6:00 p.m. The officers remained at the hospital to provide additional security.

-253-

3:45 p.m.

Officers on duty were redeployed to the following locations:

1. Two officers at 6th and Lucas Streets.
2. Two officers at Wilshire Boulevard and Lucas Street.
3. Two officers at Shatto and Witmer Streets.

    Note: These six officers were instructed to screen all persons attempting to gain access to the hospital.

4. Eight officers assigned to the main entrance.
5. Two officers assigned to the roof to maintain sniper alert.
6. Two officers at the rear portion of the hospital.
7. Thirteen officers were deployed inside at various key locations near the Senator's room.

4:00 p.m.

Sergeants J. R. Ponce and R. G. Dress, Intelligence Division, met Jacqueline Kennedy at the International Airport and transported her to the hospital. Sergeant W. B. Smith and Officer H. C. Smith assisted the Secret Service in providing security for Mrs. J. Kennedy at the airport.

6:30 p.m.

Thirty-five officers and five sergeants from Metropolitan Division, commanded by Lt. R. Tackaberry, arrived at the hospital. They relieved and assumed the duties of the Metropolitan Division day watch officers.

Tackaberry deployed seventeen officers and two sergeants on external security. The remaining eighteen officers and three

-254-

sergeants were assigned inside the hospital to assist the Secret Service with the protection of the Senator and his family.

During the remainder of the evening, security was conducted in a routine manner without incident.

June 6, 1968

1:44 a.m.

Senator Robert F. Kennedy expired. His body was transported to the "morgue room" in the basement of the hospital.

3:00 a.m. to 9:15 a.m.

Sergeant W. C. Jordan and Officer D. K. Stewart were assigned to attend the autopsy of Senator Kennedy. Security for the autopsy room was provided by Sgt. Swihart, Officers T. A. Finn, C. A. Labrow, R. Sanchez and S. K. Mills. Mr. C. Collier, Scientific Investigation Division, photographed various phases of the autopsy.

Members present from the Los Angeles County Coroner's Office included:

Thomas T. Noguchi, M.D.	Chief Medical Examiner
Herbert McRoy	Administrative Deputy
John E. Holloway, M.D.	Deputy Medical Examiner
Abraham T. Lu, M.D.	Deputy Medical Examiner
Edward Day	Senior Investigator
Richard Kottke	Deputy Coroner - Photographer
Charles Maxwell	Chief of Investigation Division, in charge of security inside the autopsy room.

Others present at various times during the autopsy were:

Maxwell M. Andler, M.D.
Henry M. Cuneo, M.D.
Kenneth Earle, M.D.
Pierre A. Finck, M.D., Colonel, U.S.A.
John E. Holloway, M.D.
J. A. Keren, M.D.
James L. Poppen, M.D.
Nat D. Reid, M.D.
Robert L. Scanlan, M.D.
Charles J. Stanl III, M.D., Commander, U.S.N.

8:30 a.m.

Sergeants B. L. Everheart and T. J. White, Rampart Division supervisors, reported with sixteen officers from various patrol divisions. They relieved the Metropolitan Division personnel and assumed their security posts.

The crowd across the street from the main entrance of the hospital was estimated at two hundred persons.

9:30 a.m.

Lieutenant B. E. Sanderson arrived and took command as senior officer-in-charge.

The crowd had now grown to one thousand persons, and another two hundred persons were reported at Lucas and Shatto Streets.

10:30 a.m. to 11:30 a.m.

Thirty additional officers and four sergeants from various patrol divisions were dispatched to the hospital to assist in crowd control.

12:30 p.m.

Senator Kennedy's body was placed in a hearse at the hospital. The hearse then joined a motorcade of twelve vehicles containing

-256-

members of the Kennedy family, staff members, Secret Service and personnel from Intelligence Division. Sergeant W. M. Sherman led the motorcade in a marked police vehicle. A second marked police car was positioned at the rear of the motorcade to prevent unauthorized vehicles from joining the convoy. Additional mobilized security was provided by ten motorcycle mounted officers from Traffic Enforcement Division.

12:33 p.m.

The motorcade departed from the hospital en route to the International Airport.

1:00 p.m.

Security at the hospital was discontinued. All police personnel were dismissed from this detail and returned to their respective Divisions.

* * * * * * * * *

CHAPTER 7

Toxicology/Coroners Report, Psychiatry, LA County DA Investigation, LAPD

Back in the day, it was common for drug users to get high on barbiturates. The first drug of choice to get high on were "reds," also known as "Red Devils" – seconal (secobarbital,) and one 100 mg capsule were enough to "get a good buzz." Second, were "rainbows" also known as tuinal which was a combination of seconal "reds" and amytal "blue angels" (amobarbital) Less frequently used were "yellow jackets" also known as Nembutal (pentobarbital) Nembutal was a very short-acting barbiturate sleeping aid, or hypnotic, and used for very short term insomnia or as an anticonvulsant drug. This was the drug that Marilyn Monroe allegedly committed "Probable Suicide," of which, as we already said, there is no such thing in the competent pathologist's vocabulary. Nembutal seldom used for long term sleeping disorders because of the addictive potential and short-lasting effects. Yes, Nembutal, the drug of choice used by Marilyn, pushed on her by Dr. Ralph Greenson and Dr. Engelberg (who was heavily influenced by Freud.) To better explain this, it's like Xanax (alprazolam) prescribed today for anxiety and panic disorders as opposed to longer, safer acting benzodiazepines (benzos) such as Clonazepam. Also, short-acting drugs, similar to Nembutal, are far more addictive, and normally used for short term use only because of misuse of a habit-forming medicine.

So why did Dr. Greenson and Dr. Engelberg prescribe Nembutal to Marilyn Monroe? Dr. Greenson believed to be one of the forefront Psychoanalysts and Psychiatrists in his era and was a learned doctor from the Freudian theories. However, this writer believes that Dr. Greenson was unethical and did whatever told to do by the CIA, Communist party, and other governmental agencies; and possibly Lee Strasberg, Marilyn's acting coach.

The rumor was that Dr. Greenson was having a sexual relationship with Marilyn Monroe (countertransference), and Robert Kennedy threatened him that "…if you don't do as I tell you,

you will lose your license and go to jail..." In one of Greenson's interview(s), when asked if Marilyn committed suicide, he said, "...ask Robert Kennedy..." Why would Dr. Greenson say this?

(As the authors of this book, an appointment was made by one author in 2001 to be a member of the County Substance Abuse Committee – after that, our committee was combined with the Mental Health board in or around 2013, to become the Behavioral Health Commission. The author has been a commissioner since 2013. With a BA in Applied Criminology, Masters in Education, Licensed California Private Investigator, Certified Medical Investigator (ACFEI), Nationally Certified Psychiatric Technician (AAPT) and the other author an AA in Business Administration, Medical Investigator Intern, Veteran Advocate; and both authors are Community Emergency Response Team members (FEMA,) Certified Peer & Family Support Specialist (NAMI), Certified "Building Sustainable Transitions of Care for People with Addictions" HMA; Certified "Applied Suicide Intervention Skills Training" RUHS - the relevance to Marilyn's substance abuse and alleged mental health issues are well versed and the credibility to make assessments well established. Also, this author investigated approximately 12 state death penalty cases up for an appeal at the United States District Court level, which required re-investigating the crime; and conducting a mitigation investigation that included interviewing the Death Row inmates relatives, three generations back to determine; physical abuse, mental illness, drug use or abuse, environmental influence, be-it contaminated drinking water, living close to toxic waste, air contamination, or the actual environment such as a gang-infested neighborhood, or poverty-stricken environment.)

TOXICOLOGY / CORONERS REPORT

How did Marilyn Monroe Die? Using the "FALSE" explanation of "Probable Suicide"?

(Special thanks to Tony Plant: Pilot, Researcher and Marilyn Monroe fan who wants the truth conveyed - the information provided by Mr. Plant has been reviewed and confirmed by a Ph.D. – Medical Lab Scientist, for accuracy, credibility, and reliability of the findings)

(NOTE: a certified copy of the Autopsy obtained from the L.A. County Coroner was used, in part, for analysis.)

As we mentioned, a certified copy of the Coroner's Report, Case Number 1962-81128, was received shortly after May 23, 2016, certified by Mark A. Fajardo, M.D., Chief Medical Examiner-Coroner. Her death, according to the Office of County Coroner, was *"Acute Barbiturate Poisoning"* – *"Ingestion of Overdose"* and labeled **"Probable Suicide."**

"Just how many drugs did they find in Marilyn's autopsy? During the autopsy, on August 6, 1962, the toxicologist Raymond Abernathy, dated August 6, 1962, found her blood concentration of "Barbiturates" to be 4.5 mg percent, this converts to 45 ppm (parts per million) however phenobarbital (phenobarbitone) is absent according to Dr. R.J. Abernathy (fig.). The supplemental, dated August 13, 1962, shows 8 mg percent Chloral Hydrate in the blood and 13.0 mg percent Pentobarbital (Nembutal) in the liver. According to the (Physicians' Desk Reference), the toxic amount of Nembutal in the blood starts at 12 ppm and increases to the "Usual Death Level" of between 1 5 to 40 ppm. This means Marilyn had more Nembutal in her blood system than the scale even shows. Almost four times the toxic level and three times the minimum amount it takes for death to occur. The autopsy shows 13.0 mg percent of pentobarbital in the liver; this converts to 130 ppm or over 10 times the amount that the blood in the body can handle. Death usually occurs at 15 ppm, Marilyn was 45 ppm. A lethal dose of Nembutal is between 2 grams and 10 grams (20-100 capsules) in the average person. Marilyn was taking 100 mg capsules, so 2 grams would be 20 capsules (or the minimum lethal dose.) So if Marilyn's blood shows to be three times the lethal amount, then that would be 60 capsules. Now add in the amount that was found in her liver to this amount = 10 times the lethal dose + 3 times the lethal dose = 13 times the lethal dose."

And the State Actors want us to believe that Marilyn died from oral ingestion of a handful of Nembutal and Chloral Hydrate capsules?

"...The autopsy shows 8.0 mg percent of Chloral Hydrate in the blood. This converts to 80 mcg/mg; according to Micromedex, the toxic level of CH starts at 30 mcg/mg and goes to the lethal level of 100 mcg/ml... meaning that she had almost three times the toxic amount of CH and just under the lethal dose. So she just 'almost' had enough Chloral Hydrate in her blood to kill her. As far as the number of pills consumed – Marilyn was taking 500 mg capsules of CH. A normal dose of CH is between 500-1000 mg. The lethal dose is considered to be 10 grams, which are 20 capsules. Marilyn had roughly 80% of the lethal dose of 20 capsule amounts in her blood, so she would have had to take 17 capsules of Chloral Hydrate..."

Two leading specialist in the field of psychoactive drug-induced deaths, psychiatrist and neurologist Dr. Louis A. Gottschalk, and toxicologist Robert H. Cravey were pioneers in developing the Standard Uniform Rating System in 1972. Their findings published in their book- Toxicology and Pathological Studies on Psychoactive Drug-Induced Death; enumerate autopsies of over 1500 frequent drug users. Every autopsy of a death caused by oral ingestion included drug analysis of the stomach contents in EVERY case large concentration to lesser amounts of the specific drug taken orally found in the stomach.' **Dr. Cravey**, quoted as saying, *"In EVERY case of a drug overdose through the oral entry, I have ALWAYS found drugs in the stomach."*

Is it possible that Marilyn had an enormous amount of drugs on hand? She would have had to been saving them from months before. According to the pharmacy invoice and the pill bottles found on the scene, we only have proof that she had 25 Nembutal capsules available to her that last week. Dr. Engelberg stated in 1962 that he gave her a prescription of Nembutal a few days before her last bottle of 25; however, the pharmacy records don't agree with this. Dr. Engelberg stated that he did prescribe Nembutal, however, not Chloral Hydrate. The bottle dated August 3rd was a refill- no; however, that bottle had a new order number, so it was not a refill. The pharmacy records can only account for 25 Nembutal. So again, who is telling the truth? She did have more than 50 Chloral Hydrate on hand, though!

Dr. Thomas Noguchi, Deputy Coroner, sent the blood, liver, kidney, stomach and contents, urine, and intestine to Raymond Abernathy, head toxicologist of the L.A. County Coroner, for testing. The testing was done under the supervision of Theodore Curphy, Chief Medical Examiner, and Coroner. In the digestive system, only the stomach and upper part of the small intestine were tested for drugs. No traces of crystals found, so Abernathy didn't test any further for drugs taken orally. Noguchi asked again for further tests, but the organs had already been thrown away, thrown away, an important case such as this one with conscience negligence? If the lower part of the small intestine showed no traces of orally taken drugs, then the next place to look was the kidney, which is where, unused orally taken drugs, would have ended up. This would be the final part of the chain before leaving the body in the urine or feces. If no traces were found in the kidneys, then it would prove Marilyn did not take any oral drugs.

Ironically, all of the toxicology tests performed was at UCLA Medical Center. Both Dr. Greenson and Dr. Abernathy were on the board there. Dr. Greenson was the last doctor to see Marilyn and admitted to giving her sedatives. Therefore, if no orally consumed drugs were found in her system, then Dr. Greenson would have been implicated.

During an interview given by the **Chief Medical Examiner and Coroner Theodore Curphy**, he said, *"...It is my conclusion that the death of Marilyn Monroe was caused by a self-administered overdose of sedative drugs; the mode of death is "Probable Suicide..."The toxicologist, Dr. Abernathy, discovered a large number of Chloral Hydrate..."* **YouTube**

Let's try to understand what we have read and documented related to the concept of Marilyn Monroe ingesting the pills orally. She didn't – her blood level had nearly four times the amount of drugs to kill her, yet they could not prove where the drugs came from, and they didn't even try to prove it. Marilyn would have had to swallow twice as many capsules as a non-tolerant person to get the number of drugs found in her system so there is no way she could have accidentally swallowed just a few too many capsules…if she would had wanted to kill herself and swallowed all of the Nembutal she could find and all but 10 of the Chloral Hydrate; with this amount, she would have died long before the entire amount had completely digested past her stomach and completely past her small intestine. We are not talking about finding the die in her stomach, but rather crystals or the drug itself. So in layman's terms, Marilyn would have taken so many capsules to kill her that there should have been a lot of drug crystals found in her digestive system. The certified autopsy report states that NO CRYSTALS were found, and as a result, the logical conclusion is she DID NOT swallow the drugs – believe it or not!...

Psychiatry and Psychoanalysis

According to the American Psychiatric Association (www.psychiatry.org), the first edition of the DSM (Diagnostic and Statistical Manual of Mental Disorders) published in 1952; DSM II published in 1968; DSM III published in 1980 – the DSM IV was published in 1994 and finally the current DSM-5, as of 2019, published in 2013. Accordingly, any diagnostic disorders assigned to Marilyn Monroe would have been found in the DSM I. In or around 1950, *"...Phillip Ash gathered data on three psychiatrists who independently interviewed and diagnosed 52 applicants to the Central Intelligence Agency (CIA). Ash was surprised by a large amount of variance among the psychiatrist in their diagnostic impressions of these different individuals. Ash concluded that psychiatric classification lacked adequate reliability when being used clinically to assign diagnoses..."* (**The Cycle of Classification: DSM-I through DMS-5, www.annualsreviews.org**)

In the 1960s, common psychoactive drugs available were amphetamine-type stimulants (Black Beauties) hypnotics such as Barbiturates, Benzodiazepines, Quaaludes, Noludar, Chloral Hydrate, Librium, Valmed, and also psychedelics. There was also pain medication such as Methadone, Darvocet, Demerol (JFK loved Demerol) Percodan, etc. However, psychotropics such as Parnate (Tranylcypromine) anti-depressant/monoamine oxidase inhibitor and Thorazine (Chlorpromazine) were developed as a true psychoactive drug in the 1950s for schizophrenia, bipolar disorder, attention deficit, nausea, vomiting, and anxiety. (Wikipedia – Chlorpromazine)

Additionally, illegal drugs such as PCP, LSD, Cocaine, Mescaline, and Glue, etc. ingested by experimental users were prevalent. Now we know by reviewing Marilyn Monroe's prescriptions and pharmacy invoice to her estate, she has been prescribed an overabundance of sedatives and hypnotics. NOTE: the quality of the prescriptions is extremely poor. However, this writer has inserted the few good quality photo's– others are in our possession:

ALL drugs listed below, prescribed by Dr. Engelberg (oh my my, did he lie?)
Information obtained from prescriptions, coroner's report and creditors claim***

November 4, 1961---Noludar, #50 (456099) Empty container: Sedative/hypnotic
Not sure who the prescriber was-

June 7, 1962----Chloral Hydrate, #100/Librium #50/Valmid #50
Chloral Hydrate: (19293/4/5) a sedative and hypnotic drug; Librium a sedative and hypnotic benzodiazepine tranquilizer; Valmid: Sedative/hypnotic used for insomnia

June 8, 1962---Sombulex,(hexobarbital) #100, prescription number (19329),
Receipt #12542 $7.75, hypnotic and sedative effect (used to murder woman prisoners at Ravensbruck German Concentration camp). Prescribed by Dr. Engelberg.

June 15, 1962---Parnate #100 (19537)
Tranylcpromine, **anti-depressant**/monoamine oxidase inhibitor
(Why did Dr. Engelberg prescribe the psychotropic & not Dr. Greenson?

June 18, 1962---Percodan #24 (19603)
Percodan: pain reliever that is a combination of aspirin and oxycodone

June 27, 1962---Lomotil #24
Lomotil: diarrhea medication that is chemically related to another opioid

July 1, 1962-----Dexedrine #12 (Script# 19974 – Order #11526)
Stimulant used as an UPPER

July 5, 1962--filled Order #11589 at San Vicente Pharmacy (unknown script)
July 10 1962---**Librium #100/ Valmid #50/ Seconal #25/ Tuinal #25**
Seconal: (Scripts #s 20198/99/20200/01 – Order #11438) an anesthetic, hypnotic, sedative barbiturate Tuinal: a sedative comprised of two barbiturates- secobarbital sodium (Seconal) and amobarbitol sodium

July 17 1962--- Redisol #36/ Hydrozets #24/ Sulfa Gum/ Darvon #24 (Script #s 320361/62/63 – Order #11252) Hydrozets: throat lozenges / Redisol: Injectable b-12 vitamins / Sulfa Gum: for sore throat

July 25 1962--- Chloral Hydrate #50/ Sulfathallidine #36 (Script # 20569 – Order # 13132 & 13137) **(creditors claim)** Sulfathallidine: pain relief/anesthetic

July 31 1962----Chloral Hydrate #50 (Script #20570 – Order # 13004) (creditors claim)

August 3 1962---Nembutal #25 (Script# 2 0858 – Order #12905)/ unidentified pink Capsules #32/ Phenergan #25(20857) Dr. Engelberg prescribed the Phenergan; and the Nembutal – **(creditors claim)** Phenergan, anti-histamine / sedative

Believed to be the total amount of drugs prescribed to Marilyn Monroe; (two month period)

June 5 – August 3 = Valmid 150
June 5 – August 3 = Chloral Hydrate 150
June 5 – August 3 = Librium 150
June 5 – August 3 = Percodan 24
June 5 – August 3 = Darvon 24
June 5 – August 3 = Seconal 25
June 5 – August 3 = Tuinal 25
June 5 – August 3 = Nembutal 25
June 5 – August 3 = Phenergan 25

(On 48 Hours: The Mystery of Marilyn Monroe's Death Investigation) Dr. Engelberg stated: "Were you aware of other suicide attempts that she made before her death? *"...I'm not aware of any deliberate suicide attempts, I was only aware of the one time when she currently had too much to drink and had taken slightly more than she should have, but that was not a serious attempt...There was quite a volume of pills discovered at her death, at her bedside".* Do you recall looking at a list of those pills, and were they all prescribed by you*?..."NO, only one had been prescribed by me; I was surprised to see at the side of her bed a large number of other sleeping pills...I knew nothing about Chloral Hydrate. I never used Chloral Hydrate..."* So you wrote her prescription for Nembutal only? *"That was it. It's the only prescription I wrote..."* **He lied – he did prescribe Nembutal, according to the prescriptions. Why wasn't this investigated?**

So, where do the 50 Nembutal capsules come into play? Did Dr. Greenson bring 25 additional capsules when he visited Marilyn on August 4, 1962 – or was it in an injectable form? The operatives/hitmen used an injectable form of Nembutal to kill Marilyn! The rest will fall into place- Additionally, if Marilyn had so many sedatives by her bedside, why did she call Jeanne Carman for more? (to this day, it is not uncommon for drug users to ask friends for additional drugs).

Interestingly, Dr. Engelberg prescribed Sombulex (hexobarbital) #100, prescription number 19329, $7.75, June 8 - hypnotic and sedative effect, and used to **murder woman prisoners at Ravensbruck German Concentration camp, WHY?**

With this said, how can we accept the methods Dr. Greenson or Dr. Marianne Kris (Marilyn's physiatrist from New York) used to diagnose Marilyn Monroe and the findings of the same? It was subjective thought and based on different theories from past "Founders of

Psychiatry" such as Freud, Jung, and others. Not really reliable, yet authors of today pretend they can make a sound judgment of Marilyn Monroe's mental "instability"; as they describe it. And some are only clinicians with a Master's Degree and probably cannot differentiate between Carl Gustav Jung and Sigmund Freud? Well, who can – the concepts of both are almost a dichotomy of thoughts and theory.

The bottom line, the major problem with Marilyn Monroe was her use of sedatives, uppers, and alcohol as opposed to some misdiagnosed mental illness. Marilyn did not take the prescribed psychotropic to help her alleged mental illness.

When you get high with **Nembutal, Seconal, Tuinal or Chloral Hydrate and Champagne** one night, then get up for work and take an upper, **Dexedrine**, a cognitive enhancer, in the morning, you will resemble characteristics of being a bi-polar or a depressed person because of the chemical imbalance and reactions of the **dopamine** in your brain…just like Marilyn. Can this author's concept be opposed? Of course – but remember the theories of Freud and Jung; this is a classic controversy of what and who is correct.

Los Angeles County District Attorney's Office

In or about March 16, 2016, the L.A. County District Attorney's Office responded to our agency request for records related to the investigation of the Marilyn Monroe death. As they state, around 1980-1982, the "first" investigation was conducted by the DA's office.

To begin with, it's interesting that the D.A.'s office could not conclude if Marilyn's body were picked-up by **Westwood Village Mortuary or the Coroner's office**. A pretty simple question, and if the DA cannot decipher this, how can we expect them to conduct a competent investigation? Marilyn's body was picked-up around 5:45 a.m. by **Westwood Village Mortuary Guy and Don Hockett, where Alan Abbott was waiting to embalm Marilyn**; however, at around 9:00 a.m. (over three hours later) her body was transferred by Coroner's officials to the County Coroner. *Where is the chain of evidence?* There is none – the chain of evidence, lost, when Westwood Village Mortuary picked up Marilyn's body, sealed the doors, and took her body to the Mortuary, and then the Coroner's office picked her up at the Mortuary; three hours later.

In theory, we can stop right here and conclude, based solely on the above paragraph, that the autopsy was completely invalid, unable to confirm accurately any findings – for instance, what if the mortuary attendant and mortician tampered with Marilyn's blood, or injected her with Nembutal or Chloral Hydrate; or at the most extreme, went to the lengths of starting to embalming Marilyn at the mortuary; the Coroner would've had to have completely fabricated their findings to cover-up the incompetent chain of command of evidence; however, we will continue and give you evidence that we believe is beyond a reasonable doubt that Marilyn Monroe was killed, 'murdered.' **(The Death of Marilyn Monroe Report To The District Attorney – Ronald H. Carroll, Assistant District Attorney – Alan B. Tomich, Investigator – December 1982 – Page 3, attached)** *"...Reports concerning the removal of the body from the scene of death on the morning of August 5 are unclear. It is unclear whether or not Marilyn's body was initially removed by the Westwood Village Mortuary and turned over to the Coroner's Office or whether the Coroner's Office took possession of the body at the scene and delivered it from there to the downtown Los Angeles facility..."* The District Attorney's office could not confirm that the Mortuary took possession of Marilyn's body directly from her home because of evidentiary problems – they knew this – so the DA's office played stupid and made the statement that *"...It is unclear whether or not Marilyn's body was removed from her home by the Westwood Village Mortuary..."* Once the chain of evidence is tainted, it's very difficult to correct the problem unless you have a time machine. Is this exculpatory evidence that was covered up to both confuse the public and keep the autopsy as legitimate as possible- even though it was a farce from the beginning?

The "Red Diary," according to the DA, was more than likely NOT a real item but rather a figment of one's imagination. However, did the DA interview the LAPD OCID officers – NO! Real shitty job by the D.A. Investigators headed by Chief Investigator Clayton Anderson (deceased.)

The DA did their best to discredit Lionel Grandison's (Coroner's Aid) assertion that the Diary did indeed exist. Was a background conducted on Mr. Grandison? Why not do the same thing on Dr. Greenson, Eunice Murray, Pat Newcomb, Peter Lawford, the LAPD OCID officers at the scene, Ray and George, as bodyguards for Attorney General Robert Kennedy. Was the DA's office so inept back then that such obvious things right in front of their face that they overlooked it?

How do we know this and confirm it in another manner; as mentioned – according to Thomas Noguchi, Deputy Coroner; **Gary Hackett of Westwood Village Mortuary, who is one of two that picked up Marilyn's body from her home at approximately 5:45 a.m. at 12305 5th Helena Dr. provided the initial information regarding the death of Marilyn and sealed the doors.** After that, at approximately 9:00 a.m. Coroner's officials *"...Bob Dambacher and Clete Pace picked-up Marilyn's body from Westwood Village Mortuary, just off Wilshire Blvd.; Dambacher said (from Tuolumne County) we checked her over thoroughly but found only one small bruise. As we were wheeling her out the door, wrapped in a sheet, there were reporters and photographers everywhere. It was a media circus, and my picture was seen worldwide all over the wire service..."* (The Union Democrat – interview published June 4, 2015)

The DA's writings on the Marilyn Monroe death investigation is potentially a great cover-up, total incompetence, or just because it was an old case and they did not want to ruffle feathers of superiors or the infamous and secretive, Los Angeles Police Department, Organized Crime Intelligence Division. The Los Angeles County District Attorney's office is an outstanding organization with superior skills. Question; was the District Attorney's office just incompetent or possibly part of a cover-up? There is information available today that the D.A.'s office did not have back in 1962 or 1982, so should we give them a reason for inaccuracy?

Los Angeles Police Department – Organized Crime Intelligence Division

The Gangster Squad was a special unit created by the Los Angeles Police Department in 1946 by Chief of Police Clemence Horrall to keep the East Coast Mafia and organized crime out of Los Angeles (Wikipedia.) Later the squad evolved to be known as OCID - Organized Crime Intelligence Division. For a better look into the OCID, former OCID Detective Michael J. Rothmiller wrote a book "L.A. Secret Police: Inside the LAPD Elite Spy Network" wow, what a compelling story. Later on, the unit became known as the Public Disorder Intelligence Division –

Marvin Iannone was the one who headed up this division, which had seen the scandal in or around 1985.

William Parker became LAPD's Chief of Police in 1950, and he expanded the newly evolved renamed OCID unit from Interim Chief William Worton. LAPD Capt. James Hamilton and Lt. Marion B. Phillips formed and expanded the OCID under Chief Parker's command.

Let's skip to the facts, and you can read more about LAPD OCID from Mike's book. **James Jarrett** was an LAPD SWAT instructor and OCID officer after leading assassination teams in Vietnam, Cambodia, and Laos; also, he had a close working relationship with OCID Officer Russell Meltzer and **Sgt. George Arnold** (paid by the CIA as assets.) Both Meltzer and Arnold (aka Arnold George Trut) supervised Jarrett's work related to an undercover operation against Don Freed and Shirley Sutherland (Friends of the Panthers.) [Reliable Confidential Informant confirmed information]

Jarrett was an alloplastic (criminality, mental illness, and activism) personality type with a sadomasochistic adventurist attitude and enjoyed planting hand grenades on suspects, assassinations, gun-runner, and breaking into homes. **(CIA in the LAPD – Sue Marshall, Los Angeles Free Press, July 1970 - attached)** Meltzer and Arnold were not far behind him in the 'kill if you have too, or just want too' mentality. There were about 10 OCID officers involved in this corrupt investigation/set-up against Friends of the Panthers; however, none of them prosecuted by the L.A. County District Attorney's office or the United States Attorney's office (AUSA's Compton and Byrne) – wonder why?

Chief Parker would do anything for the Kennedy's because he wanted J. Edgar Hoover's FBI directorship. William Parker was police corruption on steroids – this author believes he was a mentally ill man, very sick - and allegedly covered-up the murder and mutilation of Elizabeth Short – Black Dahlia murder. Another example, Parker would have OCID agents help murder Marilyn Monroe and confiscate Marilyn Monroe's phone records after her murder. One of the LAPD OCID officers was, as mentioned above, Sgt. George Arnold – more on this in the next chapter. This writer finds it a bit ironic that Parker died at an awards ceremony when he stood up and had a massive heart attack! The CIA had already perfected a gun to shoot frozen projectiles that would cause a heart attack that was unable to trace medically. Makes you wonder, did the CIA use this on Chief Parker?

There's another book out there, actually several, close in the true content of what happened to Marilyn Monroe; however, they assumed that OCID protection officers, Case and Ahern were the assassins who helped Robert Kennedy kill Marilyn – this was an assumption on their part and is completely incorrect!

ATTACHMENTS

THE DEATH OF MARILYN MONROE

REPORT TO THE DISTRICT ATTORNEY

RONALD H. CARROLL
Assistant District Attorney

ALAN B. TOMICH
Investigator

December, 1982

THE DEATH OF MARILYN MONROE

In August of this year the District Attorney directed the Assistant District Attorney to initiate a review of documents and other available materials relating to the death of movie actress Marilyn Monroe, who died in 1962. The purpose of the threshold investigation was to determine if sufficient facts and circumstances exist to warrant the opening of a full criminal investigation as a possible homicide case. There is no Statute of Limitation applicable to Murder under California law.

On the basis of our 3½-month review of printed material and interviews, we conclude that there are insufficient facts to warrant opening a criminal investigation into the death of Marilyn Monroe. Although factual discrepancies exist and unanswered questions surfaced in our probe, the cumulative evidence available to us fails to support any theory of criminal conduct relating to her death. The original Coroner's finding of "probable suicide" is reasonably supported by the data examined, although some evidence reviewed supports to a lesser degree the conclusion that the actress's death may have been accidental. An equally plausible hypothesis is that although her ingestion of a lethal quantity of barbiturates was voluntary, she may have been in such a state of emotional confusion that she herself lacked a clearly-formed purpose.

As the 20th Anniversary of Miss Monroe's death approached, several persons emerged to criticize the original police investigation of Monroe's death and to criticize the Coroner's Office's handling of the case. Most of the criticism was a repeat of allegations which were published periodically during the preceding twenty years. However, one new issue came to light when a Mr. Lionel Grandison, a Coroner's Aide during 1962, made public statements at various press conferences wherein he alleged that he had been coerced into signing the Death Certificate shortly after the autopsy of Miss Monroe had been performed, and alleged also that he had seen a red diary included in the property received by the Coroner's Office at the time the body was transported to that office, but that the diary had subsequently disappeared.

Various authors, some print media representatives, and the Los Angeles County Board of Supervisors asked the District Attorney's Office to look into the matters raised by Grandison. Grandison and an author by the name of Robert Slatzer allege that the diary contained references to sensitive government operations and references to then-Attorney General Robert Kennedy, and perhaps to his brother as well, and thus the circumstances of Miss Monroe's death might actually involve a murder conspiracy to silence the actress and prevent her from revealing either secret government operations or personal matters which might be of great embarrassment to the Attorney General or the President.

The first step in the threshold examination was to secure all existing documents from official sources. District Attorney files and archives were examined; all existing files in the possession of the Coroner's Office and the Los Angeles Police Department were requested. In addition, the United States Department of Justice was queried as were the local FBI offices.

Several agencies routinely purge files after a fixed period of time, usually ten years or less, and therefore some difficulty was experienced in attempting to recreate a complete documentation from official sources. Fortunately, many individuals who had personal knowledge of the events surrounding the death in 1962 are still alive and were interviewed. Documents reviewed included LAPD reports (some of which were reconstructed); Coroner's reports (including toxicological reports); FBI reports (although heavily censored); news reports and other publications. Forty people were interviewed in person or telephonically. The scene of death was visited, with particular attention paid to the layout of the neighborhood and the ability of neighboring residents to observe the Monroe house from the vantage point of each residence. Four pathologists were consulted, with varying degrees of particularity, including Thomas Noguchi, the original autopsy surgeon.

Outline of Known Facts Relating to the Death of Marilyn Monroe

Marilyn Monroe died on the night of August 4 or in the early morning hours of August 5, 1962. Her body was discovered by her housekeeper, Mrs. Eunice Murray.

Los Angeles Police Department reports state that Mrs. Murray telephoned Miss Monroe's psychiatrist, Dr. Ralph Greenson, at 3:30 a.m. on August 5, 1962. She told him that Miss Monroe's bedroom light was on and that the bedroom door was locked. Dr. Greenson immediately left his nearby residence and arrived at the Monroe house at approximately 3:40 a.m. He entered her bedroom through a window and there observed Marilyn lying on the bed, apparently deceased.

Miss Monroe's physician, Dr. Hyman Engleberg, was summoned to the scene and arrived there at approximately 3:50 a.m., August 5, 1962. Upon viewing the body, he immediately pronounced her dead.

The Los Angeles Police Department, West Los Angeles Division, was telephonically notified of Miss Monroe's death at 4:25 a.m., August 5, 1962. Sgt. Jack Clemmons responded to the scene. Later that morning Investigative Officer R.E. Byron was dispatched to the scene.

Sgt. Byron conducted the police investigation of the death.

The Los Angeles County Coroner's Office's reports state that that office was notified of Miss Monroe's death by Sgt. Clemmons at 5:25 a.m.

Reports concerning removal of the body from the scene of death on the morning of August 5 are unclear. It is unclear whether or not the body was initially removed by the Westwood Village Mortuary and turned over to the Coroner's Office or whether the Coroner's Office took possession of the body at the scene and delivered it from there to the downtown Los Angeles facility. The reports do state that the body was delivered to the Coroner's Office by coroner staff personnel at 9 a.m. on August 5, 1962.

At 10:30 a.m. on August 5, 1962, Deputy Coroner Examiner, Dr. Thomas Noguchi, performed the autopsy on Miss Monroe's body. He also took samples of blood and liver materials which he submitted for toxicological study. Other samples were taken and saved for future study on an as-needed basis.

The results of the blood and liver toxicological examination show that there were 8 mg. percent chloral hydrate and 4.5 mg. percent of barbiturates in the blood and 13.0 mg. percent pentobarbital in the liver.

Dr. Noguchi concluded, based on his examination, that Miss Monroe died as a result of acute barbiturate poisoning, "due to an ingestion of an overdose." Although the blood and liver toxicological studies identified the toxic level of drugs in the system, no precise estimates could be made of the number of pills ingested to reach the toxic levels in the blood and liver.

Officials of the Coroner's Office contacted the Suicide Prevention Center in Los Angeles and requested a report from a Psychiatric Investigative Team to assist the Coroner's Office in determining whether or not Miss Monroe had accidently or intentionally ingested the lethal quantities of drugs. The Suicide Team was headed by Robert Litman, M.D.; Norman Farberow, Ph.D.; and Norman Tabachnich, M.D. The Team report concluded, "On the basis of all the information obtained it is our opinion that the case is a probable suicide."

CONDUCT OF CORONER'S OFFICE

The written reports associated with the autopsy performed on August 5, 1962, were examined by an independent expert, Dr. Boyd G. Stephens, Chief Medical Examiner-Coroner, City and County of San Francisco. The Los Angeles District Attorney's Office solicited Dr. Stephens' assistance.

Dr. Stephens reports that the methodology and report itself reflect a legitimate, scientifically acceptable medical examination performed in accordance with 1962 standards for such examinations. He further

Prescription 20362

PATIENT: Marilyn Monroe
ADDRESS: 12305 5th Helena

℞ Darvon Comp. #24
One for pain
Tablet

DOCTOR: H. Engelberg M.D.
9730 Wilshire
DATE: 7-17-62
PRICE: 3.70

Prescription 20361

PATIENT: Marilyn Monroe
ADDRESS: 12305 5th Helena

℞ Hydrogets #24
Suck one q 2-3 hrs for sore throat

DOCTOR: H. Engelberg M.D.
9730 Wilshire
DATE: 7-17-62
PRICE: 4.95

Prescription 1:

PATIENT: Marilyn Monroe
ADDRESS: 12305 5th Helena

℞ Chloral Hydrate #50
  b H ? 0.5 gm
  Sig as directed
  Label
                              40 gr. tube
SIG: G5.474
DOCTOR: H. Engelberg
  9730 Wilshire
NO. 19293
DATE: 6-7-62
PRICE: 6.45

Prescription 2:

PATIENT: Marilyn Monroe
ADDRESS: 12305 5th Helena
         JA 49

℞ Dexedrine #12
  5 mgm
  One for energy
  (Tennis Club)
  phoned
  refill
  qq x —
  G3 4/30
  G5 4366
SIG:
DOCTOR: Hyman Engelberg
  9730 Wilshire
NO. 19974
DATE: 7-1-62
PRICE: 1.50

Prescription 1:

PATIENT: Marilyn Monroe
ADDRESS: 12305 5th Helena   6-15-62

19537

℞ Parnate 10mg
#100
Sig. ī tid: label

SIG: H. Engelberg, MD
DOCTOR: 9730 Wilshire
NO. 1165
DATE: 6-15-62
PRICE:

Prescription 2:

PATIENT: Marilyn Monroe
ADDRESS: 12305 5th Helena   6-18-62

℞ Percodan 24
#79
for severe pain or cramps

SIG: H. Engelberg, MD
DOCTOR: 9730 Wilshire
NO. 19603
DATE: 6-18-62
PRICE: 2.95

Prescription 1:

PATIENT: Marilyn Monroe
ADDRESS: 12305 5th Helena
No. 20363

Rx Sulfa Gum
Chew [illegible] ½ hour
6 times daily - following
gargle
Sulfa Gum

DOCTOR: H. Engelberg
9730 Wilshire
DATE: 7-17-62
PRICE: 2.75

Prescription 2:

DATE: 8-3-62
PATIENT: Marilyn Monroe
ADDRESS: 12305 5th Helena
No. 20857

Rx Phenergan 25 mg
Tab 25
Sig: i (one) sleep
3.90
H. Engelberg M.D.
9730 Wilshire Bev Hills

www.LAmorguefiles.com

PATIENT Marilyn Monroe
ADDRESS 12305 5th Helena

19329

℞ Nembutal #100

Sig. ut. label

CR 54366

DOCTOR H. Engelberg MD
9735 Wilshire

PATIENT Marilyn Monroe
ADDRESS 12305 5th Helena

℞ Valmid #50   20198   3.85
    One for sleep

label   Seconal 1½ gr #25   20199   2.35
    One for sleep

Phenergan 3 gr. #75   20200   2.45
    One for sleep

Sod. Librium 10 mgm #100   20201   12.50

DOCTOR Hyman Engelberg MD   **DATE** 7-10-62
9730 Wilshire

PATIENT Marilyn Monroe
ADDRESS 12305 5th Helena

℞ Valmid #50
1½ drachm
label

SIG: CR 5-4366   NO 19294
DOCTOR H. Engelberg MD   DATE 6-7-62
9730 Wilshire   PRICE 3.85

March 28, 1962

Miss Monroe,

Did deAngelis ever reply to you directly re what part is so around and spring which not delivered although part of original order?

The New York Times subscription for yourself up March 31 - for Dr. Greenson up April 7.... I called and re-ordered both....

You told me once for Dr. Greenson was a Xmas gift.... Am I right it's for one year...?

CIA in the LAPD???

SUE MARSHALL

A CIA penetration agent?

This was the description, conjuring up images of poisoned darts and sado-masochistic enzyme cleaners, which playwright Don Freed and attorney Luke McKissack used to describe James Jarrett, late of the LAPD and presently stationed in Israel by the Central Intelligence Agency, ostensibly to act as a saboteur. (Jarrett has worked in this capacity overseas prior to this case.)

If it wasn't for the zealous efforts of ten officers of the Los Angeles Police Department in trying to secure a conviction against Freed and actress Shirley Sutherland, the fact might never have been revealed that Jarrett (and possibly other LAPD cops) could act as a CIA agent while on the city payroll.

The Sutherland-Freed case has proved a great embarrassment to the police department and U.S. attorney's office. From Oct. 2, 1969, when Jarrett tried to entrap Freed and Sutherland by planting on Don Freed hand grenades which he had personally stolen from the San Diego Naval Armory, to December, when ten LAPD willingly complied in breaking into the home of a private investigator for the defense to steal tape recordings and papers, the actions of the police have been concretely illegal.

"I almost could say that the LAPD probably wasn't aware that Jarrett was a CIA man," Freed commented to the Free Press. "Maybe that's being naive. Jarrett has been a 'hit' man—the leader of political assassination teams—in Vietnam, Cambodia and Laos. He had worked for the CIA in Latin America. He had come to the LA police to help train the Special Weapons and Tactics (SWAT) squad, which was responsible for the raid on the Black Panther Party headquarters last December."

Even when Jarrett was working within the group called Friends of the Panthers (now known as Liberation Union) as an infiltrator— even before he was proven to be a cop of any kind—he was recognized to be an individual with serious mental problems.

"Jarrett talked freely about atrocities he had committed in Vietnam and his current life as a cat burglar and gun-runner," recalled Don Freed.

"His acting-out personality was plain. To use the psychological vocabulary, he has a allo-plastic personality. Here is a man who was emotionally battle-scarred in Vietnam, and his sickness has been channelled for the use of the CIA.

"Jarrett acts out with his body an inner world of sado-masochistic adventures which fit exactly the patter he has been programmed to follow. This is the logical step beyond drafting and brainwashing someone in the army. Jarrett is a victim, too, and his very existence demands an explanation. There are thousands of men like him returning from the battlefields; beneath their clean-cut blonde exterior they are walking schizophrenics—and monsters.

"When Jarrett was in Friends of the Panthers, I maintained that he was sick and should not be rejected. Jarrett ran tight, effective self-defense and first aid classes. He was skilled and patient and revealed a helpful, friendly side in direct contrast to his usual provocative behavior."

In September, one of the young women belonging to the Friends was raped by reactionary Cubans. Jarrett suggested that mace be obtained for the women to carry for self-defense. Freed agreed.

On Oct. 2, the day before Freed was scheduled to go to New York to supervise the Broadway opening of his play, "Inquest; the United States vs. Julius and Ethel Rosenberg," Jarrett delivered a brown cardboard box which was supposed to contain mace to Freed;s home at 4:15 a.m. About 4:30, detectives arrived simultaneously at two homes, to hold guns to the head of Don and Barbara Freed, Shirley Sutherland and her three young children. Don Freed Shirley Sutherland were arrested for possession of hand grenades,

and held on $25,000 bond to face a ten-year prison sentence.

When the case came to trial Judge Warren J. Ferguson of the United States Federal Court dropped all charges in view of the obvious entrapment. The U.S. Attorney, however, in an unprecedented move, appealed the judge's decision!

But even more colorful things were to come.

Luke McKissack, chief Southern California counsel for the Black Panther Party, had been retained by Freed and Sutherland for their defense. In many of his celebrated cases, such as the Sirhan Sirhan defense, McKissack has retained the services of private investigator Mike McCowan.

McCowan comes uncomfortably close to the mod-squad stereotype of what a "private dick" should be. He is a licensed private investigator, a lawyer, a ladies' man, and a Gemini. Being a ten-year veteran of the police department himself, McCowan accepted the fact that one of his assistants, Sam Bluth, was a former LAPD officer who had been canned from the force for minor infractions.

Apparently, Sam Bluth dug being a cop to the extent that he would break the law to get back in.

According to a Memorandum of Fact submitted to the court by the U.S. Attorney's office, the following facts came to light while Sutherland and Freed were awaiting trial.

On Dec. 10, 1969, Sam Bluth visited the Venice Police Department and conferred with a Lt. Hegge. The content of their conversation (this is from the U.S. Attorney, remember) was a meeting that Bluth had observed where Don Freed and Shirley Sutherland had discussed James Jarrett.

Lt. Hegge sent Sam Bluth to the glass house downtown where he laid his scene on Inspector McCalley, Lt. Loomis of the Internal Affairs Division and Sgt. Sandlin and Officer Vincent Kelly of the Intelligence Department. Bluth produced tapes containing recorded conversations between the defendants and investigator McCowan. The police made copies of these tapes. Later that day, Sgt. George Arnold and Sgt. Jack Guterding listened to the three hours of tape Bluth had provided.

The next day, Arnold and Guterding followed Bluth to Mike McCowan's apartment, in the hope of finding more information. Bluth broke in, and returned in 20 minutes with further information.

On Dec. 15, three days later, Jarrett, Officer Russell Meltzer and Sgt. Arnold listened to McCowan's tapes. Meltzer and Arnold had supervised Jarrett's work in LAPD capacity when the hand grenades were delivered to Don Freed in October, and these three policemen served as prosecution witnesses.

On Dec. 31, Bluth supplied Arnold and Guterding with several hours more of stolen tapes.

On Jan. 5, Bluth met with Sgt. Fier of the LAPD Intelligence Department and gave him a 15-20 page transcript with more information regarding the Sutherland-Freed defense.

In March, Mike McCowan, Luke McKissack, Don Freed and Shirley Sutherland submitted simultaneous lawsuits against the City of Los Angeles in an amount totalling one million dollars. They are charging the police department with Theft of Property, Invasion of Privacy, Interference with Business Relation, and Abridgement of Constitutional and Civil Rights.

In the suit, the four defendants charge that Sam Bluth and the ten police officers "entered into a scheme...to knowing and intentionally steal...and aid and abet the theft of claimants' property, work product, and confidential information relating to the (Sutherland-Freed) defense...defraud (the claimants) and to pervert and obstruct justice...."

In all, nearly 20 specific violations of the Penal Code are alleged in the suit.

Luke McKissack and Mike McCowan have actively demanded that the U.S. Attorney's office seek indictment against the ten policemen

CIA agent James Jarrett (center) flanked by LAPD cohorts. Photo by Gilbert Weingourt

named in the suit at the time it was filed last March, but the U.S. Attorney's office has so far failed to respond.

"I consider this case sort of a reverse of the Friar's Club case," remarked Mike McCowan. "In that instance, the attorneys and defendents were indicted under an archaic rule that says attorneys can't have copies of a Grand Jury transcript. Here we have specific evidence of a crime committed on behalf of the prosecution, and Buck Compton and Matt Byrne (U.S. Attorney's office) have done nothing to these individuals who disclosed the entire case for the defense, I think it's shocking."

"What this case spotlights is one of the major problems of this society," stated attorney McKissack. "The police are too busy enforcing laws against others to let themselves be governed by these same laws.

"Here we have an open and shut case of numerous grave and felonious offenses committed by these ten police officers — and some of them are from the higher echelons of the LAPD. One would think that the relevant processing agency, the U.S. Attorney and the LA District Attorney, would take action, as they undoubtedly would against John Doe Citizen were he to precipitate the same crime.

"The police, of course, by virtue of their fraternization with this prosecuting agency, are immune to retribution for their infractions.

"What does one do when you have an uncontested expose of crimes by law enforcement officers and NO ONE WILL TAKE ACTION? Police who seek to flaunt the very laws they ostensibly cherish will undoubtedly gain solace from the Freed-Sutherland debacle."

CHAPTER 8

The burden of Proof, the Pilot, False Information, Wiretaps, and the Doctors

Let's start by explaining the types of evidence it takes to prove murder, sometimes known as the burden of proof. In a civil court arena, the standard of findings is **"preponderance of the evidence,"** which is 51% wins over 49%. Next, we have **"clear and convincing"** evidence which is sometimes used in administrative courts or hearings and has a range of around 80% more likely than not; and the strongest findings is "beyond a reasonable doubt," the words speak for itself; no other real explanation overbears the findings. However, there have been convictions of murder and other serious crimes using circumstantial evidence and does not meet the **"beyond a reasonable doubt"** legal mindset.

Was Peter Lawford directed by the British Secret Service to act as an agent? Being Peter Lawford was the liaison between the Kennedy's and Winston Churchill; Lawford had no problem conveying information he learned from the Kennedy's to his London controller ~ handler. How do we know, Top Secret documents reveal these findings? If you look, you will find it!

The Pilot, the helicopter, and the plane

Now here are some controversial things that happened, yet some may disagree with our findings. We will include documents where we can, and hopefully will help corroborate our message to the public. Joe Hymans, a reporter for the Los Angeles Tribune, interviewed neighbors of Peter Lawford, who stated they saw a helicopter land on the Santa Monica shore behind Peter Lawford's beach house very early on August 5, 1962. Neighbors also called the police and complained about sand propelled into their pools. Billy Woodfield, a photographer, and journalist located records of the Connor Helicopter Service of Santa Monica, which showed that a passenger had been picked-up at Lawford's house at 2:00 a.m. Sunday, August 5, 1962. **Pilot Hal C. Conners, a DOD advisor,** was the President of the Helicopter Association International in 1961. Hal Connors owned a Bell 47 H, later known as Connors Air Taxi Service, housed at Santa Monica Airport CA; formerly Clover Airfield, a military base until Santa Monica purchased it. One of Hal Connors pilot's**, Judson B. Stevens,** worked for Hal and piloted the Bell 47 H helicopter and also fixed-winged aircraft. This author spoke with Tess Stevens, Judson Stevens Widow, and she confirmed to us the connection with Marilyn Monroe and that Judson would fly Robert Kennedy to and from different places; Judson worked for Connor Helicopter Service and Connor's Air Taxi at Santa Monica Airport. We requested a copy of Judson's flight logs for **August 4, 1962, and August 5, 1962**; however the only thing we received back from his widow, **Tess Stevens, was a handwritten note - attached**"*…we have no air logs and cannot determine dates…here is a list of other pilots that may be of value…*" **James J. Zonlick** was the Chief Pilot who also worked for Hal Connors – we interviewed his ex-wife by telephone; Betty; she told us that James often spoke about flying Robert around and mentioned the Marilyn Monroe event the night of August 4 and 5, 1962, and other occasions.

We have a good authority that OCID operatives picked-up Robert Kennedy on August 4, 1962, from the **Santa Monica Airport (according to Dan Stewart LAPD OCID – Hardcopy)** around 1:30 p.m. and took him to Marilyn's. (Confirmation in the next chapters) We also know a fixed-wing aircraft, or military helicopter, flew into Santa Monica Airport from **Hollister Airport**, CA – Hollister operated as a military base until June 1946 when civilian activity was allowed. Hollister is only 15 miles from Gilroy, CA. and has two runways, 3,000 ft. also 6000 ft. As you may remember, Robert Kennedy said he was staying at the Bates Ranch located in Gilroy. Robert Kennedy also used the family aircraft, a Convair 240 - N 240 K - called the "Caroline" named after JFK's daughter, many times. Many credible witnesses have stated that Robert Kennedy was in Los Angeles on August 4, 1962. We have solid information that Robert Kennedy was able to fly from Hollister to Santa Monica in a fixed-wing aircraft in approximately 1 hour. Kennedy was at Marilyn's and orchestrated the murder of Marilyn

Monroe using Dr. Greenson and the two OCID operatives Ray Cadena and George Arnold. I understand that Peter Lawford hid in the closet -

FALSE INFORMATION

Intelligence agencies are overseen by the 'Director of National Intelligence,' next on the list is the NSA – National Security Agency, probably more ethical than the others; Then we have the CIA, Central Intelligence Agency, with rouge agents, mentally ill operatives and most of them trained in one of two courses; a six-week course or six-month course, at Camp Peary (the FARM) in hypnotherapy, to kill without feelings of remorse, they teach you how to deceive, role play, psychologically assess, sell, exploit – the black arts, not witchcraft but rather a trade-craft, and a whole bunch of other operational tactics. Allegedly they cannot operate within the United States boundaries – right! As we head down the pyramid, the next agency is the FBI, Federal Bureau of Investigation. Well, we know from current history the only ethical agency is the NSA – in fact, it was Admiral Rogers, Director, NSA, 2016, who informed President Trump that he was under surveillance while running for president and thereafter…why because it was illegal!

The CIA and MSM became one in the same many years ago, with former operatives becoming television journalists – and I use the term journalists very loosely because most of them are incompetent left-wing nut cases told what to say. Whether you believe in the CIA's MK-Ultra or not, the MSM journalists are a product of mind control and fear control and will say whatever told to say – and also remember money talks!

Another story promoted, yet flawed in many ways, was the ambulance driver James Hall – he used an alias with the L.A. County D.A.'s office as Rick Stone. **(Memo dated 8/16/82, page 3 of 4 - attached)** James Hall said the CIA was involved, and he was in fear of his life, so he planned to meet with an L.A County D.A. Investigator in Las Vegas. He also said he went to the Monroe residence on August 5, 1962, between 4:00 a.m. and 6:00 a.m. – (no way – the mortuary picked up her body at 5:45 a.m., and no heart needle entrance observed on Marilyn Monroe's body during the autopsy – Hall stated that Dr. Greenson injected a heart needle to revive Marilyn. Also, Hall initially wanted compensation from the DA for his testimony while using his alias. A bit odd and zero credibility!

According to documents within the LA County District Attorney's file, Lady Mary Lawford, Peter Lawford's mother's home, was broken into on August 3, 1962- why? It was never looked into by law enforcement according to our search records. We understand that Lady Lawford, later killed, because she was a threat to the Kennedy's and knew many secrets from her son and the British Secret Service.

WIRETAP

Marilyn Monroe's home wiretapped, as well as Peter Lawford's beach house. By Hoffa, the FBI, CIA, and others, Marilyn's home, wired to the max, was an eavesdropper's dream. Wire tappers who worked for Bernard Spindel, the expert in the field of wiretapping, along with a few of his employees listed below, were the culprits. In 1966 after an investigation of Spindel by the Manhattan District Attorney's Office, a warrant was served on Spendel, and 29 others were arrested for wiretapping. According to the Los Angeles District Attorney's Office, evidence was seized, including tape-recordings which were subsequently placed in an evidence vault and sealed by the court. **(Memo by DA Investigator Al Tomich, dated September 3, 1982 – file number 82-G-2236 - attached)** Bill Graff, Chief Investigator, US Environmental Protection Agency, stated, *"...prior to Spindel's arrest, Spindel had suggested to Graff's informant (deceased) that he (Spindel) had tape-recordings of conversations regarding Monroe and Robert Kennedy... Graff stated that if Monroe's residence was "bugged" that the eavesdropping expert on the West Coast was Harold Lipsett...Lipsett was associated with Spendel and was a co-defendant on Spindel's case..."* this was a 1968 conviction.

Fred Otash left several boxes of information to his daughter Colleen. The Hollywood Reporter got access to the files, as Fred stated in writings: "...I listened to Marilyn Monroe die...she was passed around like a piece of meat, it was a violent argument about their relationship and the commitment and promises he made to her. She was screaming, and they were trying to quiet her down. She's in the bedroom, and Bobby gets the pillow, and he muffles her on the bed to keep the neighbors from hearing; she finally quieted down, and then he was looking to get out of there..."

Reed Sutton Wilson One of the brightest and gifted electronic experts there was. His aptitude was superior to any wire-tapper around, back then and even today, if he were alive. As quoted in his Obituary published **in (the Santa Barbara News-Press Online Edition from August 6 to August 10, 2015 - attached)**: *"...the high and mighty came to Reed. He worked for U.S. presidents and would-be presidents, heads of state, the government's most secret agencies, the moguls of the entertainment industry, some of the men who once ruled Las Vegas, and powerful companies the world over..."*

Retired LAPD OCID Sgt, Scherrer, and Reed were good friends when they lived in Solvang and associated at the La Cumbre Country Club. They would talk about the good-old-days and operations they worked on together. A confidential source (intelligence operative) told me directly, that Reed was outside of Marilyn's home on August 4, 1962, in a truck with electronic equipment, and heard the murder in real-time, with Robert Kennedy, Dr. Greenson, Peter Lawford, OCID agents Cadena and Green, as they committed the act. Reed was told to stand-down by the agency he was working for and did so reluctantly because he was an ethical man with a conscience. His recordings are one of several sets of tape recordings related to the evening of August 4, 1962. Transcripts also exist and are available for a price $$

Harold K. Lipsett intervened by Clayton Anderson, Chief L.A. CO. D.A. Investigations **(September 14, 1982,** telephonic interview memo dated September 15, 1982 - attached) wherein Lipsett stated, *"...he did not know Bernard Spindel...nor did he ever have, nor did he ever hear any tape recordings concerning Marilyn Monroe, the Kennedy's or anyone else associated with Marilyn Monroe..."*

Maybe, just maybe, Clayton Anderson did not ask the right questions? Lipsett was co-defendant on Spendel's case? Another liar and cover-up person with ties to the CIA?

John Dansford was an average private investigator with average skills related to surveillance and wiretapping. He worked for Fred Otash and did a lot of the mundane work others would not do, like listen in while Robert and Marilyn were doing the wild thing –moans groans and all.

John Broady - listed by Harold Lipsett as a friend of Spendel's – Broady set-up an eavesdropping nest in an apartment in Midtown Manhattan in the mid-1950's – "…he used to spy on a rogue Chinese Airforce general who'd stolen millions from the US Government…"

The DOCTORS & PLAYERS

Dr. Milton Wexler, Psychologist, California license number 374, an associate of Greenson;

Dr. Ralph Greenson, M.D. California license number A6753, born Romeo Samuel Greenschpoon, a Communist Sympathizer – Marilyn Monroe's Psychoanalyst- Ironically, Dr. Greenson manipulated Marilyn Monroe to move close to his home to help gain control of Marilyn; Greenson purchased his home from Eunice Murray who worked for Marilyn at the request of Dr. Greenson. **(The Reporters – Marilyn Monroe, A case for Murder YouTube)** When asked if Marilyn Monroe was killed? Greenson says, *"…ask Robert Kennedy…"* Greenson was at Marilyns the night of August 4, 1962, actually several times. Greenson was also part of the cover-up and participated in the murder. **(LA DA #49, page 2 - attached)** *"…Greenson advised Dr. Litman that on Friday, August 3, 1962, he had a lengthy visit with Monroe. On Saturday, August 4, 1962, he received a telephone call from her during the late afternoon and arranged to visit her at her residence. He arrived at the residence at about 5:00 p.m. and remained until after 7:00 p.m…."* Dr. Greenson was likely in contact with Attorney General Robert Kennedy during this time and throughout the incident.

Dr. Hyman Engelberg, M.D. California license number A7462 – a Communist Sympathizer; Marilyn Monroe's internist, Lied on a recorded interview stating he did not prescribe Chloral Hydrate –look at the prescriptions…he also was part of the cover-up and lied to the LAPD with completely false exculpatory information to mislead the public and above-board law enforcement agents. Dr. Engelberg was an identified Communist!

Dr. Lee E. Siegel, M.D. California license number A6470 – Twentieth Century Fox doctor – also treated Marilyn with "vitamin shots" and Benzedrine; also a few prescriptions of Nembutal

Dr. Robert E. Litman, M.D., Psychiatrist, California license number C7905 – According to the LA-CO DA's office, Dr. Litman interviewed Dr. Greenson on August 7, 1962 (**LA DA #49, pages 1, 2 - attached**) – *"...Dr. Greenson, who related that in 1959, Monroe was referred to him by Dr. Kris, a New York City Psychiatrist. Dr. Greenson described her (Monroe) as having an extremely weak psychological structure. She felt unimportant and insignificant and was extremely impulsive- during this time Monroe dated some "very Important and powerful men." Dr. Greenson would not identify the men and be concerned she was being used in these relationships. Monroe appeared gratified to be associated with such powerful and important men..."* **On page 3, 3rd paragraph,** Dr. Litman stated, *"...The best inference is that she ingested approximately 25 100 mg. Of Nembutal capsules and approximately 20 Chloral Hydrate capsules around 9:00 p.m. ..."* **Gee, could these "very Important and powerful men." be Robert Kennedy and Jack Kennedy?**

Dr. Marianne Rie-Kris, M.D. Psychiatrist, New York license number 041050, date of licensure: 11/16/1942   - According to documents and writings, Dr. Kris committed Marilyn to the Payne-Whitney psychiatric hospital against her will. Additionally, Dr. Kris lived at 135 Central Park West, Langham building. the same building where the Strasberg's lived (Marilyn Monroe's acting coach) – odd. They were the major recipients to the proceeds in Marilyn's Last Will & Testimony, written approximately three weeks before Marilyn was committed to the NYC's Payne-Whitney Hospital, on or about February 5, 1961. Marianne Kris told Marilyn that she was going to a private hospital for rest. A Payne Whitney intern told Marilyn - "You are a very, very sick girl. And you've been sick for a long time." So who was sick and medically unethical, Dr. Kris, friends with Anna Freud, or Marilyn Monroe?

As you can see for yourself, and decipher, Marilyn Monroe had the odds against her – yet she still functioned well under the circumstances and hurdles she had to cross. After reviewing Marilyn's last will, it appears as though questions arise about the authenticity of the signatures and also the witnesses. Wonder why no one has raised this question or looked further into the possibility of civil or criminal acts related to the will?

ATTACHMENTS

MR. GENTILLALLI

WE HAVE NO AIR LOGS & CANNOT DETERMINE DATES

HERE IS A LIST OF OTHER PILOTS THAT MAY BE OF VALUE

T. STEVENS

JUD STEVENS

LOS ANGELES COUNTY DISTRICT ATTORNEY
BUREAU OF INVESTIGATION

INVESTIGATOR'S REPORT

REPORT MADE BY:	DATE:	CHARGE:	FILE NO.
Al Tomich	8/16/82	187 P.C., Murder	82-6-2236

SUSPECT:	COMPLAINANT:
unknown	Assistant District Attorney Ronald Carroll
	VICTIM: Marilyn Monroe

SYNOPSIS OF FACTS:

Case opened 8/16/82, date last report 8/16/82 (Request for Investigation). Anonymous informant contacted complainant regarding sale of information contrary to news accounts of victim's death. Informant demanded expense money for preliminary interview plus an undisclosed amount of money for his testimony. Expense money refused; informant states he will sell information to tabloid. Informant will telephone complainant in several days for possible changes. Totally, three telephone calls received. Last telephone call received indicated he would not require any expenses to provide information.

PENDING

On August 13, 1982, at approximately 9:30 a.m., Assistant District Attorney Ronald Carroll received a telephone call from an anonymous source, who stated that for the purpose of the call he would use the alias of Rick Stone.

The telephone call was received in Asst. D.A. Carroll's office, Room 18-107, Criminal Courts Building, 210 W. Temple Street, L.A., telephone 974-3508, and was tape-recorded. The tape is retained by the Sound Lab under file #82-538CO.

Stone stated that at the time of Marilyn Monroe's death, he was employed by California Ambulance Service. He described the location of the ambulance service as Santa Monica Blvd., just inside Santa Monica city limits.

Stone stated that between approximately 4:00 a.m. and 6:00 am he and an attendant were dispatched by the West Los Angeles Police Department to Monroe's residence, which was located on a street that he referred to as one of the Helenas. The Helenas were a series of small streets and were numerically numbered.

Upon their arrival, Stone observed a female standing in front of

DISTRIBUTION:	CONTENTS NOTED
3 B	
1 DA	

Monroe's residence, hysterically screaming, "She's dead; she's dead; I think she's dead."

Stone advised the woman he would do the best he could. Stone stated the woman appeared to be a housekeeper or secretary. Stone entered the front door of the residence, took a few steps inside and then turned left and walked directly into Monroe's bedroom. The bedroom door was open at the time. He observed Monroe lying nude across the bed in a supine position with her head hanging over the edge. He threw her onto the floor and began "closed chest massage." He didn't know if she was dead, but was sure rigor mortis was not present.

Approximately three to four minutes after his arrival in Monroe's room, his partner arrived with a resuscitator. Walking directly behind his partner was a man dressed in a business suit and tie, carrying a doctor's-type medical bag. The man stated he was Monroe's physician.

The man advised Stone to put an airway into Monroe's throat and apply "positive pressure." The man then began closed chest heart massage while Stone began mouth to mouth resuscitation. Stone stated purge began emitting from Monroe's mouth. He stopped and told the man he wanted to switch procedures. The man stated, "Wait a minute," and withdrew a "loaded syringe from his bag." The man then counted down several ribs, injected the needle into the area of Monroe's heart, and discharged the contents of the syringe. The man resumed close heart massage for several minutes and then stated, "I've got to put on a show." The man then stated he was pronouncing her dead and that Stone and his partner could leave. Stone and his partner left the residence at this time.

Stone stated he was at Monroe's residence approximately fifteen minutes. He also stated that as he departed the residence it was just beginning to become daylight.

Stone described Monroe's bedroom as having a nightstand next to the bed. On top of the night stand was a telephone with the receiver in place. Also on the nightstand were pill bottles which were neatly arranged. Stone did not observe pills on the floor as reported by the press. There were no indications anyone other than the screaming woman had been inside the bedroom prior to Stone's arrival.

Stone stated he was afraid and was not relating the information to our office as a good Good Samaritan. He would require expense money for his testimony, but had no specific amount in mind. He stated he and his family were "starving to death."

He stated he was afraid because Monroe was John F. Kennedy's girlfriend and that "now you're talking about everybody dying."

Stone stated he could prove he was an ambulance driver at the time of Monroe's death. He doesn't recall the attendant who accompanied him to Monroe's residence, but was able to name the following ambulance employees who worked with him: (phonetically)

1. "Lucky", manager
2. Joe Tarno or Tarnowski, dispatcher
3. Merrell
4. Tom Fears

Stone was agreeable to an interview with an investigator and submitting to a polygraph examination. He suggested the meeting place as Las Vegas because of the 24-hour activity.

Stone was advised to telephone Asst. D.A. Carroll's office at 10:30 a.m. that day and that an investigator would speak with him regarding an interview.

On August 13, 1982, at approximately 11:20 a.m., Stone telephoned Asst. D.A. Carroll's office. Investigator Tomich was not present at the time and the call was received by Asst. D.A. Carroll. The conversation was tape recorded and the tape is retained by the Sound Lab, #82-562CO.

Stone stated he had spoken to several people and was extremely paranoid. He further stated the "C.I.A." was involved and that they have the capability of tracing telephone calls throughout the country. Asst. D.A. Carroll advised him that investigator Al Tomich would be handling the interview. Stone stated he didn't know Tomich and that he (Tomich) could be anyone. Stone was requested to speak with Inv. Tomich in order to establish Tomich's identity and recognizable appearance. Stone re-emphasized his paranoia and stated he would call Monday between 9:00 a.m. and 9:30 a.m.

On Monday, August 16, 1982, at approximately 9:20 a.m., Stone again telephone Asst. D.A. Carroll's office. Inv. Tomich received the telephone call and tape recorded the conversation. The tape is retained by the Sound Lab, #82-563CO.

Stone stated he was willing to cooperate, but that the economy had "flattened out" for him and "that for this type of information, you're going to pay." He stated he would take a polygraph examination and that upon determination of his truthfulness he would demand immediate payment.

He estimated his travel expenses in the amount of a "couple thousand dollars." The expense would include rooms, travel fare and the salary of his bodyguards. He insisted that bodyguards be present during the interview with investigator.

Stone was advised travel expense could be arranged, but that payment for the information would be determined after the information was reviewed by district attorney staff. Stone agreed, but insisted on expense money and his selection of a meeting place.

Investigator advised Stone that his demands would be considered and that he should telephone this office at 10:30 a.m. the same day. The conversation was terminated at this time.

On August 16, 1982, at 10:22 a.m., Stone telephoned Asst. D.A. Carroll's office and spoke to Inv. Tomich. The conversation was tape recorded and the tape is retained by the Sound Lab, #82-563CO.

Stone was advised that he would be required to cover his own expenses and that payment for the information would be made at a later date. Stone replied the conditions were unacceptable and that he would sell his information to a tabloid newspaper. He stated he would telephone Mr. Carroll's office in a couple of days for any changes.

Stone was asked for an approximate sale price of his information. He laughingly stated the price of the information was in excess of $500, but later stated he might not ask anything since he would receive payment from other sources.

On August 17, 1982, at 9:50 a.m., Stone telephoned Asst. D.A. Carroll's office and left a message with his secretary, Grace Kaulia. Stone stated he would provide the information to our office with no obligation or cost. He further stated he would re-call Mr. Carroll in a couple of days.

PENDING

LOS ANGELES COUNTY DISTRICT ATTORNEY
BUREAU OF INVESTIGATION
INVESTIGATOR'S REPORT

REPORT MADE BY:	DATE:	CHARGE:	FILE NO.
AL TOMICH	9-3-82	187 P.C., MURDER	82-G-2236

SUSPECT: UNKNOWN	COMPLAINANT: ASST. DIST. ATTORNEY RONALD H. CARROLL
	VICTIM: MARILYN MONROE

SYNOPSIS OF FACTS: Case opened 8-16-82, date last report 8-31-82. Manhattan District Attorney's Office contacted regarding disposition of tapes seized during Spindel's wiretapping arrest. A search of their vault revealed no tapes. Investigating officer on Spindel case contacted regarding same. Investigator has no knowledge of disposition of tapes, further, that a review of tapes revealed no mention of victim or association with Robert Kennedy.

PENDING

Information supplied to the District Attorney's Office alleges Bernard Spindel (deceased) tape-recorded telephonic conversations concerning Marilyn Monroe and Robert Kennedy.

On or about August 10, 1982, Assistant District Attorney Ronald Carroll telephonically interviewed David Cunningham, Chief Investigator, Manhattan District Attorney's Office, telephone (212) 553-8823. Cunningham stated that Bernard Spindel and 29 other persons were arrested for wiretapping. Part of the evidence seized during the case included tape-recordings which were subsequently placed in an evidence vault and sealed by the court. Cunningham will search the court records for the tapes and then notify Assistant D.A. Carroll of the results.

On September 2, 1982, Cunningham telephoned Assistant D.A. Carroll and stated that a search of the vault for Spindel's tapes produced negative results. He explained that ordinarily evidence is destroyed after ten years. Cunningham referred Assistant D.A. Carroll the investigating officer, Bill Graff, telephone (703) 557-7410.

On September 3, 1982, investigator telephonically interviewed Bill Graff, Chief Investigator, U.S. Environmental Protection Agency, EN 329C, 401 "M" Street S/W, Washington, DC. The interview was tape-recorded and the tape is retained by the sound lab, # 82-608CO.

Graff stated that prior to Spindel's arrest, Spindel had suggested to Graff's informant (deceased) that he (Spindel) had tape-recordings of

DISTRIBUTION:
3 - BUREAU
1 - DDA

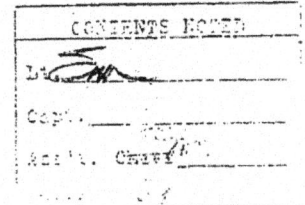

conversations regarding Monroe and Robert Kennedy. Graff stated Spindel was a known boaster and eluded to having knowledge of a number of secrets. Spindel lived in a rural area 65 miles north of New York City and was believed to have buried and hidden tapes throughout his property.

Graff further stated that an unknown number of tapes were seized during search warrants. Upon review of the tapes by his subordinates, no tapes were discovered relating to Monroe. Graff recalled that the tapes that were seized contained attempts by Spindel and company to record admissions from U.S. Marshals concerning the Hoffa trial.

Graff stated that the tapes were retained by the court after Spindel's trial and that he has no knowledge of their disposition. Graff was unable to recall the names of the subordinates that reviewed the tapes but will notify this investigator if he does.

Graff stated that if Monroe's residence was "bugged" that the eavesdropping expert on the west coast was Harold Lipsett. Lipsett was associated with Spindel and was a co-defendant on Spindel's case.

PENDING

Reed Sutton Wilson

Passed away on July 31, 2015 aged 83, in Solvang. Reed was born December 13, 1931 in Washington, D.C., to Gertrude and Harry Sutton Wilson. The youngest in a family of three, he attended Avondale Military Academy middle school in Virginia, then Woodbridge High School in D.C. From early childhood, he evinced an innate ability in electronics - the expertise that was to make him a legend in his time in his profession and beyond.

When he was still a toddler, Reed's parents were astonished to find that he had repaired a broken set of Christmas tree lights. By the time he got to elementary school he was helping out in a radio repair shop. Using the discarded parts he salvaged, he was soon building his own radio systems and police monitors. His room at home was a clutter of wires and electronic equipment, and his family nicknamed him "Radar." By the time Reed was in high school, he had graduated to repairing TV's and had fellows working for him. Not content with electronics, he was photo editor of his high school magazine and freelanced for local newspapers. Thanks to the police radio that he installed in his first car, he would often get to the scene of an incident before the police - and grab the photographs.

It was the police who first took note of Reed's aptitude for designing and building electronic equipment and his talent for problem-solving. They soon had the young man designing specialized equipment and advising on evidence. Then, in his early twenties, he discovered Los Angeles - when it was a place of true glamor and innovation. Though he would travel frequently back and forth, never letting go his East Coast contacts, the move to LA marked the real beginning of his career in highly-specialized equipment design.

Reed's genius - and it was that - was to take him to every corner of the United States and far beyond: south of the border, to the Middle East, and South-East Asia. He became the electronic go-to man for devices to enable the tracking of stolen goods, for systems - long before GPS - to locate kidnap victims, for tailing devices, for whatever magic the client required and the technology of the day made possible.

The high and the mighty came to Reed. He worked for US presidents and would-be presidents, heads of state, the government's most secret agencies, the moguls of the entertainment industry, some of the men who once ruled Las Vegas, and powerful companies the world over. An anti-eavesdropping system that Reed designed was installed in boardrooms worldwide.

In recent years, family and friends encouraged him to write his memoirs. The facts, people would tell him, were important for the historical record and could do no harm now. Reed would think about it, on occasion be tempted, then decline. He had usually promised a client confidentiality, and it was important to him to keep his word. As important, evidently, as all his technological expertise.

Away from the electronics and the secrets, there was another, physically-gifted, Reed. He played baseball at the Military Academy, was a pretty wicked "side-armed" pitcher, and an avid swimmer. Later in life, he took up skiing, water skiing and tennis, and excelled in them all. In 1988, when Reed and his wife moved to Santa Barbara, they joined the Tennis Club of Santa Barbara and made lasting friends. At La Cumbre Country Club, to which they eventually migrated, Reed enjoyed his "Old Guy Tennis".

Reed is survived by Benita, his wife of 46 years, his love, his partner and his soul mate; by his daughter Karen and son-in-law Pete, and granddaughter Michelle of Newbury Park; by his daughter Kim of Arkansas; by his grandson Jeffrey Reed and his granddaughter Renee Alice, and their parents Doug and Donna of Santa Barbara; by his granddaughter Destiny Rose and her parents Debbie and Rod of Paso Robles; and by his nieces, Roni, Donna, Kim and Alexis, all of northern California.

A Memorial Service will be held at 4:00 PM Sunday, August 16, at the La Cumbre Country Club, 4015 Via Laguna, Santa Barbara. Please RSVP to hillside44@aol.com

In lieu of flowers, donations may be made to ASAP of Goleta or Wildlife Care Network, Goleta.

Published in The Santa Barbara News-Press Online Edition from Aug. 6 to Aug. 10, 2015

MEMORANDUM

TO: ALAN B. TOMICH
             Investigator

FROM: CLAYTON R. ANDERSON, Chief
             Bureau of Investigation (974-3601)

SUBJECT: TELEPHONE INTERVIEW OF HAL LIPSET

DATE: SEPTEMBER 15, 1982

On September 14, 1982 I telephonically interviewed private detective Hal Lipset, principal of Lipset and Associates, San Francisco, California. Mr. Lipset stated that he did not know Bernard Spindel, although he knew who he was. Lipset stated that he was once called by a New York lawyer who represented a paranoid woman. The lawyer indicated that Spindel was receiving a large continuing fee from the woman because he, Spindel, told the woman her telephone lines were tapped and was constantly searching for the "bug". Lipset stated that he checked out the woman's telephone lines and determined there was in fact no tap on the lines. Mr. Lipset stated that he was acquainted with an associate of Spindel, a man named John Broady. Lipset indicated that was the extent of his "association" with Spindel.

Lipset stated that he did not have, nor did he ever have, nor has he ever heard any tape recordings concerning Marilyn Monroe, the Kennedys or anyone else associated with Marilyn Monroe.

ch

LOS ANGELES COUNTY DISTRICT ATTORNEY
BUREAU OF INVESTIGATION
INVESTIGATOR'S REPORT

REPORT MADE BY:	DATE:	CHARGE:	FILE NO.
AL TOMICH	10/8/82	187 P.C., MURDER	82-G-2236

SUSPECT:	COMPLAINANT: ASST. DISTRICT ATTORNEY RONALD CARROLL
UNKNOWN	VICTIM: MARILYN MONROE

SYNOPSIS OF FACTS:

Case opened 8/16/82; date last report 10/7/82.
Dr. Litman interviewed regarding findings related to victim's death by psychiatric investigative team. Dr. Litman stated victim apparently committed suicide.

PENDING

On October 8, 1982, investigator interviewed Robert E. Litman, M.D., at his office, 1041 Menlo, Los Angeles, telephone 826-1882, 386-5111. Present during the interview was Investigator Robert Seiler.

Dr. Litman, and Dr. Norman Farberow, Ph.D., were requested by L.A. County Coroner Thomas Curphey to "reconstruct the life situation of the deceased and make an inference regarding the intent of Miss Monroe, when she ingested the capsules of sedative drug(s) which caused her death." On August 15, 1962, Dr. Litman prepared a summary report of their findings and submitted it to Dr. Curphey.

Dr. Litman stated the majority of the report was based on his interview with Monroe's psychiatrist, Dr. Ralph Greenson (deceased). Dr. Litman also interviewed Dr. Engelberg, Monroe's personal physician; Dr. Lou Siegel, a studio physician; and several psychiatrists who worked at Payne Whitney Hospital, New York City, while Monroe was a psychiatric patient at Payne Whitney in the 1950's.

On August 7, 1962, Dr. Litman interviewed Dr. Greenson, who related that in 1959 Monroe was referred to him by Dr. Kris, a New York City psychiatrist. Dr. Greenson described her as having an extremely weak psychological structure. She felt unimportant and insignificant and was extremely impulsive. She derived self-confidence from her beauty and her acting, the only two things which were important to her. She felt that everyone was taking advantage of her and used her for their own purposes; financial, sexual, and publicity. Monroe suffered from insomnia for which she had taken every kind of sleeping pill. She had taken sedative drugs for many years.

DISTRIBUTION:

3 Bureau
1 DDA

During the last year of Monroe's life, she was living in Los Angeles and Dr. Greenson was her only psychiatrist. He saw her frequently, usually seven times a week. Dr. Engelberg, M.D., was brought in to try to help her wean herself off the sleeping pills. Both doctors were apprehensive that she might accidentally overdose on sleeping pills. Monroe had previously overdosed several times on barbiturates. During the Spring of 1962, Dr. Greenson arranged for a psychiatric nurse/companion, Mrs. Murry, to reside with Monroe.

During this time Monroe dated some "very important and powerful men". Dr. Greenson would not identify the men and was concerned that she was being used in these relationships. Monroe appeared gratified to be associated with such powerful and important men.

During the last month of Monroe's life, Dr. Greenson felt she was improving greatly in her ability to sleep without barbiturates or Chloral Hydrate, her two main sleeping aids.

Unknown to Dr. Greenson, Monroe obtained sleeping pills from two doctors who did not know she was getting pills from the other one. She received a prescription for 25 Nembutal capsules from Dr. Siegel which was filled on August 3, 1962 and found empty in her bedroom on August 5, 1962. Dr. Engelberg prescribed 50 Chloral Hydrate capsules which was refilled on July 31, 1962. Only 10 of the Chloral Hydrate capsules remained on August 5, 1962.

Greenson advised Dr. Litman that on Friday, August 3, 1962, he had a lengthy visit with Monroe. On Saturday, August 4, 1962, he received a telephone call from her during the late afternoon and arranged to visit her at her residence. He arrived at the residence about 5:00 p.m. and remained until after 7:00 p.m. She reportedly "let off steam" about the previous night's activities and had considerable dissatisfaction with the fact that she was the most beautiful woman in the world and did not have a date for Saturday night.

Mrs. Murray was going to spend the night at Monroe's residence. Dr. Greenson suggested that Monroe take a ride, maybe to the beach. He felt uncomfortable about having to leave her but he had another engagement that he could not break, at approximately 8:00 p.m. Monroe telephoned Dr. Greenson and advised him that she was feeling better.

Dr. Greenson was summoned to Monroe's residence at 3:00 a.m. Sunday, August 5, 1962. He went to the home, saw the locked door, broke in the window and found Monroe dead.

Dr. Litman re-interviewed Dr. Greenson on August 14, 1962. Dr. Greenson stated that for practical purposes, Monroe was taking almost no sleeping pills in July 1962. Further, that she was not a drug addict. She was aware of the dangers associated with sleeping pills but liked the "womby tomby" feeling that large amounts of sleeping pills produced. Dr. Greenson believed that due to Monroe's method of obtaining sleeping pills, she may have been accumulating them for a suicide attempt.

Dr. Greenson received information from the East Coast that on the evening of August 4, 1962, Monroe called Peter Lawford. She expressed her feelings of rejection, being ignored and abandoned. Lawford became upset and attempted to contact people in Los Angeles who might help her.

Dr. Litman summarized his report by stating Monroe was "a very dependent woman, who felt abandoned by the men in her life. She had secretly and through some subterfuge obtained a large and lethal stock of Nembutal and Chloral Hydrate. The best inference is that she ingested approximately 25 100 mgs. Nembutal capsules and approximately 20 Chloral Hydrate capsules around 9:00 p.m. Los Angeles time and lay in a coma for four to five hours before she expired." Dr. Litman believes she knew that the amount of drugs that she ingested was lethal.

Evidence in favor of suicide was the high barbiturate level, the empty bottle, the locked door, and the absence of confusion and disarray in the room.

Dr. Litman provided investigator with a report of his (Litman's) interview with Dr. Greenson and a copy of the summary report sent to the Coroner's Office. The summary report related the following:

"During the last two or three weeks of July, Dr. Engelberg, who was in charge of the prescription of medication while Dr. Greenson handled the psychotherapy, began to cautiously try out nembutal again to help Miss Monroe sleep.

A prescription for 25 gr.1½ capsules of nembutal was given miss Monroe on July 25th, and it was refilled August 3rd."

Dr. Litman's report to investigator related the following:

"She received a prescription for 25 Nembutal tablets from Dr. Siegel (filled August 3, 1962 and found empty in her bedroom) and 50 chloral hydrate capsules refilled July 31, 1962 from Dr. Engelberg. There were 10 chloral hydrate capsules remaining."

Copies of the above reports are maintained in the investigative file.

On October 18, 1982, investigator telephonically reinterviewed Dr. Litman regarding the discrepancy as to which doctor prescribed Nembutal for Monroe. Dr. Litman stated that during his interview with Dr. Greenson, Greenson stated that Engelberg had prescribed the Nembutal.

Dr. Litman interviewed Engelberg, who stated he may or may not have prescribed the Nembutal.

Dr. Litman also interviewed Siegel, who stated he may have prescribed the Nembutal.

PENDING

CHAPTER 9

<u>August 4, 1962, the last day our Marilyn was with us</u>

Marilyn's last day on earth with us – so very sad that corrupt agents, politicians, and just pure evil people took this beautiful soul from us. Why, and who did she hurt? She was always a caring and loving woman with tender thoughts and a kind spirit. We have come to learn that kindness and goodness are not a reason for God to let us live. God has given every one of us free will to do as we want ~ good or bad. However, this time, the truth has surfaced; and presented to the proper authorities review. The wrongdoers will pay for her demise either here or in the afterlife. Let's begin our walk through the injustice and scary, sick people who killed Marilyn Monroe, .may they rot in hell!

Marilyn had plans for **Monday, August 6, 1962, at 5:00 p.m.** to meet with Arthur Jacobs and J.Lee Thompson to talk about a new project, "I Love Louisa."

Marilyn planned to meet with Milton Rudin at his office on **Monday, August 6, 1962**, about the new contract with Fox studio for re-starting the shooting of "Somethings Got to Give." (They re-instated her and that gave Twentieth Century Fox rights to her life insurance policy…premeditated?

Marilyn made plans to go to New York on **Thursday, August 9, 1962**, to meet with Jule Styne regarding a song composed for the movie "I Love Louisa."

Does this sound like someone who is contemplating suicide? Regarding the walls in her room being bare, no pictures, and no furniture in her bedroom – as the "Suicide Team" addressed as a sign of suicidal tendencies –Marilyn was starting to decorate her first home on August 4, 1962, Marilyn received several items that arrived to decorate her home. The suicide team, in our humble opinion, was incompetent halfwits doing as told to do, sick bastards! Should suicide have been ruled out? Because they had a title and degree did not mean they were ethical and competent.

On August 3, 1962, Marilyn asked Pat Newcomb to come over. Pat explained that she was ill from bronchitis; however, Marilyn suggested that Pat come over and rest at her place in the solarium, and Pat agreed. After Ms. Newcomb finished work, she went to Marilyn's and food was ordered from Brigg's on August 3rd, at the cost of $49.07. (Creditors claim No. P-458935) However, Pat Newcomb told L.A. CO. D.A. Investigator, Al Tomich, during an interview on September 7, 1982 *"... Monroe and Newcomb went to a restaurant in Brentwood or Santa Monica the evening..."* of August 3, 1962. Newcomb described Monroe's mood *"...as very up and laughing..."* (**DA memo 9/7/82 – attached**)) That evening, Eunice Murray went home for the night, and both Pat and Marilyn went to bed early. Was Pat misleading the investigators; Do you think Pat would've gone out for dinner with Marilyn if she was indeed truly sick?

On Saturday, August 4, 1962, Marilyn woke up early; however, Pat slept in late. Eunice Murray arrived between 8:00-8:30 a.m. Eunice dropped her car off at a repair shop, Henry D'Antonio's auto repair, went to Marilyn's, and her vehicle was returned later that afternoon to Marilyn's.

Sometime between 9:00 a.m. and 10:00 a.m., photographer Lawrence Schiller went to Marilyn's to discuss the photo's she had taken related to the Playboy magazine. Marilyn used a pencil to mark a few that she either liked or disliked, and they decided to finish the discussion on Monday, August 6, 1962. Marilyn Monroe had a lot more to accomplish during the week of August 6, 1962 (more in the next chapter.)

Robert Kennedy flew into the Santa Monica Airport on the Convair 240 - N 240 K – fixed-wing aircraft called the "Caroline" or an Army Helicopter used for the Attorney General as needed, from Hollister Airport, CA. Keep in mind Robert Kennedy had access to aircraft to destinations of his choice. Hollister was just a few miles from Gilroy, CA, where Robert was staying at the Bates Ranch from August 3rd – August 6^{th,} 1962. Our agency is still waiting for the FAA records or additional information from the JFK Assassination Library related to the pilot log and the stewardess log or notebook. **Unidentified photographer, Black and white negative, The 'Caroline' form the Smithsonian Institution Archives, Acc. No. 11-008, Image Number: OPA-1124-15A - attachment.**

Sometime between 2:00 p.m. and 2:30 p.m., on August 4, 1962, Bobby Kennedy arrived at Marilyn's home with his brother-in-law Peter Lawford. According to the OCID officers,

here's what happened; Both LAPD OCID officers Ray Charles Cadena and George Arnold followed Lawford and Kennedy to Marilyn's home and surveilled the location. As we mentioned, the house was wire-tapped, and as we also mentioned, Ray Strait stated, as was heard on the eavesdrop tapes. Eunice answered the door and said - *"...oh, Mr. Kennedy, she's been sleeping, and he said, well I need to talk to her! "...On the tapes, I (Ray Strait) heard Robert Kennedy, the first time he came to Marilyn's house, was early in the afternoon, and it was a very amicable visit, they were having a good time drinking, and I think they were doing a little bit of smooching, it sounded like smooching, but you know, sounds can be deceiving...";* Robert Kennedy told Marilyn it was over between them and not to call him or his brother. Robert and Lawford left Marilyn's home, and Robert Kennedy checked into a local Hilton Hotel. Robert Kennedy called Dr. Ralph Greenson and threatened him to make things right, go to Marilyn's and convince her to produce her diary and not to disclose anything about the Kennedy Brothers to anyone.

Around **2:00 p.m., Joe DiMaggio Jr. called Marilyn,** collect; however, Eunice Murray told him she was not available. Joe called again around **4:30 p.m**. and again could not speak with her.

Dr. Greenson, by his admission and the LA-CO District Attorney's records, visited Marilyn at her home from approximately **5:00 p.m. to a little after 7:00 p.m.,** and this took place in her bedroom. There's confirmation by Pat Newcomb in her DA interview, **(DA memo 9/7/82 – attached),** and she also stated that when Dr. Greenson exited Marilyn's bedroom, he told Pat *"...he thought it would be better if she left..."* Wonder why – because Pat would have been another witness and possibly prevented the murder, Pat Newcomb went on to say she *"...believes Monroe's death was accidental. Monroe had plans for the following week and was not depressed about her future. Newcomb was aware that Dr. Engleberg was to advise Dr. Greenson when Monroe requested medication. Newcomb heard from an unknown source that Monroe's last prescription by Engleberg was not reported to Dr. Greenson because Engleberg was having "other problems and forgot"*

Around **7:30 p.m. Joe DiMaggio Jr.** was finally able to speak with Marilyn for about 10 to 15 minutes.

Jose Balanos called Marilyn Monroe at 9:30 p.m. on August 4, 1962; he was calling from a bar inside Ships Restaurant close to her home. Allegedly when interviewed by Anthony

Summers, Balonos stated, *"... Marilyn told me something shocking – something that one day will shock the world..."* after about 10-15 minutes into the call, Marilyn told Jose to hold on; I hear something in the guest cottage – she never returned...There are transcripts of this call, yes, transcripts of the recorded call!

According to the tapes, and biographer Richard Buskin, **at approximately 9:45 p.m., eyewitnesses saw Kennedy return – at that time, Marilyn was on the phone in her bedroom with screenwriter and Director Jose Balanos**

At approximately 9:45 p.m., in the guest cottage/room were **Robert Kennedy, Dr. Ralph Greenson, Peter Lawford, LAPD OCID officers Ray Cadena and George Arnold**. Marilyn went to the guest's cottage, and the five of them were there. The OCID operative(s) received needle(s) filled with Nembutal from Dr. Greenson, and he instructed them to inject Marilyn in her armpits with one or several doses in different areas of her underarm hair follicles. Remember, Marilyn was already sedated and submissive to the operatives. As Marilyn slipped into a coma, the operatives dragged Marilyn to her bedroom and laid her face down. Could this be what caused the bruise on her back? Picture this – one operative is carrying her legs and the other carrying her arms – she hits the floor and her back bruises? Could this have been a set- up, and they staged her body on her bed in the bedroom. After a few moments, they decided what steps to take and how the cover-up was going on, then all of them quickly left the residence. They all left before Eunice returned home at 10:30 p.m. Robert Kennedy and Dr. Greenson went with Peter Lawford, and the OCID operatives also left.

However, this sets the state of mind and also gives us a timeline: Rusty heard, on the tapes, Kennedy and two of his aids; Kennedy's LAPD OCID / CIA bodyguards searching for something in the guest house, Peter Lawford was also there with Bobby: Rusty states: *"...so Marilyn comes into the scene, and you could hear her, and she's been drinking, and her voice was slurred; she wanted to know, what are you back here for, I thought you were leaving, and she had a conversation, and she said all you people do is use me, all you want to do is use me you don't care about me, you just want to use me, and I'm tired of being used – those were her exact words-' I'm tired of being used,' and let me tell you something buster, what I know would make the headlines, and Bobby Kennedy told her, you know, you better keep your mouth shut if you know what's good for you 'I know what's good for me, I'm Marilyn Monroe, and you're not fucking with some extra here'* he said *I know who I'm dealing with, but you don't know who you are dealing with..."*

Then Otash heard, according to Richard Buskin, Bobby say, *"...give her something to calm her down..."* which is when things turned to the dark side of the story! Rusty said, *"...you could hear them smother her, you two be careful with the pillow, ah, watch out for the shots..."*

Marilyn most likely died between 10:00 p.m. and 10:20 p.m. on August 4, 1962! Marilyn's body temperature, the fact that rigor mortis had set-in, and the number of drugs in her blood and also her liver helps with the calculation of this time frame. Also, the Mortuary men, father, and son, Hockett's, stated that they had to push hard on Marilyn's arms and legs to get her on the stretcher because Rigor Mortus had already set in at approximately 5:40 a.m. August 5, 1962, when they picked up Marilyn from her home.

Around 10:30 p.m., Eunice Murray returns home with the handyman and sees Marilyn comatose or dead – she contacted Dr. Ralph Greenson. Dr. Greenson, in turn, called Arthur Jacobs, Marilyn's publicist, who handled Marilyn's press relations, and he was at the Hollywood Bowl with his wife, Natalie; Natalie was interviewed by **Hardcopy – 1962 Investigation into the death of Marilyn Monroe 2/4** – she said: *"...I think it was midway way, approximately 10:00 – 1030, I cannot say of course I don't remember exactly, but during the performance, he (Arthur Jacobs) received the news that she had died, and I didn't see him for three days..."* Makes one wonder, could Jacobs had possibly gone to the Mortuary before her body went to the coroner, and before the autopsy, or did he go to her home to help set the scene up?

Again, as detailed before, Beverly Hills Police Officer Lynn Franklin interviewed by Bill Bixby (**the Marilyn Monroe Files Live 1992 on video**) said, **a few minutes after midnight on August 5, 1962** *"...I stopped a late-model Lincoln travailing in Beverly Hills East Bound on Olympic boulevard traveling 75 miles an hour in a 25 mile an hour zone; driving the car was Peter Lawford whom I have known for a number of years and seated in the front with him was a man who I later identified as Dr. Greenson, Marilyn Monroe's Psychiatrist, and in the back seat was the Attorney General Bobby Kennedy..."*

Between 12:25 a.m. and 1:15 a.m. Robert Kennedy picked up his belongings at the Hilton Hotel with Lawford and Greenson and then went to Peter Lawford's home. Peter is all shook up, and he calls Fred Otash to go to Marilyn's and sanitizes the house. **(Attachment)**

The OCID officers called their OCID counterparts and supervisors, and along with Dr. Greenson, Dr. Engleberg, and Eunice Murray, the house was completely wiped down, and the evidence set-up to look like Marilyn Monroe committed suicide. It's possible that LAPD OCID, Marvin Iannone, helped with the clean-up and set-up? Let's face it, it's been over 57 years, and no one, no one, has unraveled this convoluted conspiracy to kill Marilyn Monroe. May Marvin have been there before LAPD Officer Clemmons arrived and then appeared and told him to leave?

Around 2:00 a.m. on August 5, 1962, pilot Hal Connors' picked up Robert Kennedy at Peter Lawford's home at the beachfront in his Bell Helicopter and flew Robert to the Santa Monica Airport. From there, Robert Kennedy flew back to Hollister Airport and then a 15-minute jaunt back to Bates Ranch. He could easily have slipped back into Bates ranch by **3:45 a.m. on August 5, 1962,** at the latest. Everyone at the ranch was adamant that Robert Kennedy never left and was there to go to mass in the morning. Great alibi, however, too many credible people saw Robert Kennedy in Los Angeles on August 4, 1962 – and at Marilyn's the evening, the homicide occurred.

What you have read is a solid, mostly confirmed timeline with documents and testimony – not a conspiracy! Marilyn Monroe's death certificate should be changed to "homicide." Also, Marvin D. Iannone, LAPD OCID retired operative needs to be interviewed or questioned before a Grand Jury. Pat Newcomb should be questioned before a Grand Jury regarding her knowledge of what happened and who was involved. They are both still alive and will likely shed light on this murder. The DA can grant them immunity in exchange for their testimony to help solve this case. They are percipient witnesses and could be held criminally liable to a certain degree; however, their knowledge would be put to better use to clarify and confirm the findings in this book, and clear-up many of the unknown questions.

This is not legal advice as I am not a lawyer – in fact, any inference to legal advice is moot and denounced as legal advice by the authors in this entire writing!

So let's hope and pray the few witnesses alive will come forward and clear their conscience before their demise. *"...it's not what you know; it's what you can prove..."* This book has taken a while to complete – documents were held up, requests went unanswered, our life has been turbulent. But we have a great God, and his good angels have protected us and allowed us to uncover some of the most interesting facts that prove Marilyn Monroe's death was not a

"Probable Suicide," and her death is not in vain. Please stand with us to compel the prosecutorial agencies to do their job – there's no statute of limitations on Homicide, so it's time to open up a very simple investigation, be truthful, and pursue lady justice. As a country, we need to heal from many wrongdoings, and this is a start. **"Her Lips Were Sealed until Now!"**

ATTACHMENT

LOS ANGELES COUNTY DISTRICT ATTORNEY
BUREAU OF INVESTIGATION

INVESTIGATOR'S REPORT

REPORT MADE BY:	DATE:	CHARGE:	FILE NO.
AL TOMICH	9/7/82	187 P.C., MURDER	82-G-2236
SUBJECT: UNKNOWN		COMPLAINANT: ASST. DIST. ATTORNEY RONALD H. CARROLL	
		VICTIM: MARILYN MONROE	

SYNOPSIS OF FACTS: Case opened 8-16-82, date last report 9-3-82. Pat Newcomb, Monroe's press agent, interviewed regarding Monroe's mental state, drug habits and romantic association with Kennedys. Newcomb related Monroe not depressed, no known drug habit or romance with Kennedys.

PENDING

On September 7, 1982, Assistant District Attorney Ronald Carroll and Investigator Tomich interviewed Patricia Newcomb at her residence, 9540 Hidden Valley Road, Beverly Hills, telephone 275-4581; Business: Rogers and Cowan, 9665 Wilshire Boulevard. Beverly Hills, telephone-same. Newcomb has recently married Gareth Wigan, a Ladd Production executive.

Newcomb stated that she was Monroe's press agent for the last two years of Monroe's life. During this time she had a "business relationship" with Monroe. Newcomb was employed by Art Jacobs who assigned her to Monroe as a press agent.

Newcomb stated Monroe was a very secretive and suspicious person. Monroe did not relate any romantic relationships with John or Robert Kennedy to her. On an unknown date, Newcomb attended a party at Peter Lawford's residence at which Monroe and Robert Kennedy were present. Newcomb stated many celebrity guests were present at the party.

Newcomb is a personal friend of Pat Lawford and met the Kennedy family through her. Newcomb has not seen Lawford for several years and believes Peter and Pat Lawford are separated.

Newcomb stated she never saw Monroe under the influence of drugs nor did she observe her taking any drugs.

On Friday, August 3, 1962, Newcomb spent the night at Monroe's residence. Monroe had suggested the visit because Newcomb had complained of bronchitis and Monroe had a heat lamp. Monroe and Newcomb went to a restaurant in Brentwood or Santa Monica that evening. Newcomb described Monroe's mood as "very up" and "laughing". They returned to Monroe's residence after

DISTRIBUTION:	CONTENTS NOTED
3 - BUREAU	Lt.
1 - DDA	Capt.
	Ass't. Chief

dinner and Newcomb spent the night.

Newcomb states that she slept in late on Saturday morning, August 4, 1962. Monroe was in a "grouchy" mood and related she hadn't slept well that night. Newcomb stated Monroe appeared angry at her because she (Newcomb) had slept late although Monroe's anger was clearly not brought on by Newcomb's sleep. Newcomb does not know why Monroe was angry with her at the time.

Newcomb spent Saturday at Monroe's residence, utilizing the sunlamp. She can't recall specifically, but believes she and Monroe ate lunch together. During the late afternoon, Newcomb observed Dr. Greenson arrive at Monroe's residence and enter Monroe's bedroom with Monroe. Dr. Greenson subsequently exited the bedroom and told Newcomb he thought it would be better if she left. Newcomb left Monroe's residence at this time.

Newcomb doesn't recall any other visitors at Monroe's residence on Saturday, August 4, 1962. Mrs. Murray, Monroe's housekeeper, was the only other person present at the residence that day.

At approximately 4 a.m., Sunday, August 5, 1962, Newcomb received a telephone call from Micky Rudin at her residence. Rudin, Monroe's attorney, advised that Monroe had overdosed on pills and had died. Rudin further advised Newcomb, "You better get over here."

Newcomb drove alone to Monroe's residence and arrived at approximately 4:30 a.m., 8/5/62. She did not observe the body and stated the scene was pandemonium. She believes the police were there and that the body was possibly being removed. Newcomb became upset at the numerous photographs being taken of her by the press and she advised them they were "vultures" and returned to her residence.

Newcomb remained at her residence for the following two days, answering numerous telephone calls. She then went to Hyannis Port at the invitation of Pat Lawford. She subsequently returned to Los Angeles and then left a short time later to attend a film festival in Venice. David Selznick requested Newcomb to accompany his wife, Jennifer, to Venice and paid for Newcomb's passage. Newcomb emphasized she received no money from the Kennedy's

Newcomb returned to the United States and during May, 1963, began employment with the U.S. Information Agency. She denied that Robert Kennedy had provided her with the job. She knew an employee of the Agency, George Stevens, and stated she was hired on her own merit based on her contacts with the film industry.

Newcomb does not recall Monroe mentioning Ted Jordan or Robert Slatzer. She described Murray as different and strange. Murray never rose her voice which Newcomb considered hard not to do around Monroe. Newcomb had no knowledge that Murray was a psychiatric nurse. Newcomb related Monroe's closest confidant was possibly Monroe's masseur, Ralph Roberts. Roberts is believed to be currently employed as an actor in New York.

2

During the interview, Newcomb was asked if she was aware that an electronic eavesdropping device which was allegedly discovered in Monroe's residence after her death. Newcomb appeared surprised and concerned as to which room was "bugged".

Newcomb believes Monroe's death was accidental. Monroe had plans for the following week and was not depressed about her future. Newcomb was aware that Dr. Engleberg was to advise Dr. Greenson when Monroe requested medication. Newcomb heard from an unknown source that Monroe's last prescription by Engleberg was not reported to Dr. Greenson because Engleberg was having "other problems and forgot".

PENDING

Today it is IMPORTANT to choose YOUR INVESTIGATOR with as much care as you choose your doctor or lawyer

for confidential service ... & discretion

FRED OTASH

INTERNATIONALLY KNOWN PRIVATE INVESTIGATOR

★ Licensed & Bonded ★ Service 'Round the Clock

Serving the Entertainment Industry for 17 Years

Member:
- California Association of Private Investigators
- Council of International Investigators
- Ten Years on Los Angeles Police Force

CIVIL — CRIMINAL — MARITAL

Investigations in strictest confidence

FRED OTASH DETECTIVE BUREAU
1342 N. LAUREL AVE., HOLLYWOOD 46, CALIFORNIA

OL. 6-4477   HO. 7-1885

"The Caroline"

CHAPTER 10

The Fascination and Legacy of Marilyn

Before 57 years ago today, in 2019, as we write this – Marilyn Monroe was extremely passionate about her love for life. Let's share some cheerful highlights of what Marilyn's life was like on her last day. We touched on some factual conspiracy on August 4, 1962; this was one of Marilyn's better days.

Although she didn't sleep well on August 3, upon awaking August 4, she was in good spirits, happily looking forward to returning to work. She was re-signed with a 20th-century fox just three days prior. Ironically, they approached her with a better salary, better deal, and she was anxiously looking forward to returning to work.

During the late morning of August 4, 1962, Marilyn received the night table she had ordered at the Mart and began to place the few pieces of furniture that also arrived from Mexico- with the help of Pat Newcomb. All of the items were going in her home, including items to go into her bedroom. In part, the reason you see Marilyn's bedroom not decorated; no pictures hung on the walls, with only minimal furniture. This could be one of the reasons the coroner's suicide team remarked (their analogy about Marilyn being depressed, possibly suicidal, making no sense what-so-ever).

On the morning of August 4, some plants and flowers were sent to her residence. She had ordered them from Frank's Nurseries and Flowers only a few days prior. She had planned to have them planted around her property to brighten it up for a special event a few days later, to potential and hopeful remarriage with Joe DiMaggio. The photo shows Eunice Murray standing in front of the plants, still wrapped in cloth waiting to be planted. Marilyn ordered Begonias, Valencia oranges, Mexican lime, and other plants categorized on a receipt and delivered to her home on August 4, 1962. After that, Pat and Marilyn rested at her poolside. She also spoke with her one of many photographers; however, they decided to continue on the following Monday to select her photos. We can say, *"Marilyn loved the camera, and the camera loved her back."*

Marilyn Monroe – First Meeting (photographer George Barris)

"The first meeting is when I went to the see of her location. I walked up two flights of stairs and I entered the room, and there I saw Marilyn leaning out the window, so our first meeting was not face to face, but her derriere to me, and I thought it was cute so I started to click the camera, she heard the noise of the camera, she turned around, she smiled at me, and she says "I'll take a dozen of those," and that's how I first met Marilyn Monroe."

The personal moment Marilyn came into our lives

Gladys – Marilyn's Mother - was born on May 27, 1902, in Piedras Negras (at that time called Porfirio Diaz), Coahuila, Mexico, to Otis and Della Monroe (this is possibly the reason why Marilyn took a great interest in and loved Mexico and its culture.) At the age of fifteen, Gladys married **Jasper Newton Baker** (aka) **Jap Baker**. Jap Baker was approximately sixteen years her senior. He was known to be an abusive man – at least this is what some biographers have said. Shame on us if he wasn't! Gladys and John had two children together named Robert and Berniece (Marilyn's half brother and sister); their marriage lasted five years from 1917-1922. Jap Bakers' birthplace was in Knox City, Kentucky, in 1886, and his date of death was September 1951, in Knox County, Kentucky.

Grace Goddard Notes On Behavior Of Marilyn Monroe's Mother

Reads *"(I wrote these things down as Gladys said them while she was staying with me), Grace Goddard."* The notes were then presumably sent to Monroe as they were among her belongings at the time of her death. The list, numbered from 1 to 15, is essentially a portrait of someone *suffering from mental illness, including paranoid delusions: "2. She thinks she was sent to State Hospital because years ago she voted on a Socialist ballot at Hawthorne and was being punished for doing so."; "6. She is being punished because years ago, she took a drink of liquor (during prohibition) and should have been sent to jail."; "7. Sleeps with her head at the foot of the bed so as not to look at Marilyn's picture - they disturb her."; "10. After listening to a political speech, she said she was needed in Russia to help them."; "11. Wishes she never had had a sexual experience so she could be more Christ-like."; "15. Misplaces or losing her glasses, watch, gloves, or other possessions and either accuse someone of stealing them, or are to blame for her losing them."* She also expresses a sudden aversion to meat and fish, fear of Catholics, believe that she was a nurse working for the government while at "Agnew" mental hospital, and belief that nobody should listen to the radio because the people are drunk when they go on air, among many other observances. This is a fascinating firsthand account of Monroe's Mother directly from someone witnessing and documenting her behavior

The Day a Star was Born

It was Tuesday, June 1, 1926; a star was born! Gladys Monroe gave birth to Norma Jeane Mortenson at the Los Angeles County hospital in California. Unbeknownst to us, it would be the arrival of the world's most glamorous icon (This might sound like a saying, but it's a fact)

On Marilyn's birth certificate, **Edward Mortenson** is listed as her Father. However, during Gladys' three-year marriage, officially finalized and divorced from Mortensen at four years (October 1924-1928), it is alleged that Gladys had an affair with 'her partner' Stanley Gifford. It is believed that when Gladys informed Stanley Gifford that she was pregnant with Norma Jeane, (Marilyn), Stanley Gifford deserted Gladys Christmas Eve 1925. Many biographers believe Norma Jeane's biological Father was Charles Stanley Gifford, a worker at the studio where Gladys worked as a film cutter. No paternity testing or DNA to confirm one way or the other was available back then. Marilyn's birth certificate lists Gladys' second husband, Martin Edward Mortenson, as the Father. While Mortenson left Gladys before Norma Jeane's birth, some biographers think he was the Father. In an interview with Lifetime, James Dougherty said, "...*Norma Jeane believed that Gifford was her Father...*" Whoever the biological Father was, he played no part in Marilyn's life.

A bit more about **Charles Stanley Gifford**, as we mentioned, he began working with Gladys at RKO consolidated films. Stanley's ex-wife, Lillian, charged Stanley Gifford with addiction to narcotics, claims of abuse, and that he associated himself with women of low character. He settled in Riverside County, California, and initially became the owner of apartments and was also successful at the Red Rock Dairy in the 1960s, back when dairies had a drive-through to make it convenient to purchase products without going to the market. The authors visited the site where the dairy was, however, track homes are there now. Dairy employees remarked that Marilyn would drive through occasionally while on her way to Palm Springs, California, in hopes that Stanley Gifford would be there to fill her order. Marilyn's gut feeling was that Stanley Gifford was her Father; deep down inside, Stanley reminded Marilyn of Clark Gable, who she genuinely took a liking. Was Mr. Gifford the Father of Marilyn Monroe? Both Gladys and Marilyn believed it to be Gifford – The absolute truth remains a mystery. Gladys was very much in love with Stanley and in hopes that they would mutually settle down and raise baby Marilyn together as a family. It was stated, that Gladys kept a photo of Stanley in their home and shared it often with Norma Jeane, as Gladys told the child that this was her Father. Stanley had no contact with Norma Jeane, and Stanley moved on and remarried. Meantime, Marilyn tried many times to contact Gifford thought the years, to no avail - leaving Marilyn feeling abandoned. Gladys was deeply upset, being Stanley was not even at the hospital during the birth of Norma Jeane; also, allegedly, Gladys left behind his other children. Stanley Gifford's birthplace was in Newport County, Rhode Island, in 1898. He died in 1965 in Hemet, Riverside County, California, USA

Gladys' third husband was **John Stewart Eley** – it's reported they got married on April 20, 1949. Not much talked about John Eley, Gladys' last husband. No direct information about his parents, siblings, or other relatives is available; however, through a cursory search, a Social security number of 518-05-0317 did appear.

Fact is, there is proof that Marilyn had written her Mother Gladys a check dated July 25,

1952, completed fully in Marilyn's handwriting to Mrs. Gladys P. Eley for $150.00. The check

was signed on the back by Mrs. Gladys P. Eley This Marilyn Monroe 1952 signed check to her

Mother, sold for $6,400 at auction. This check also is an expression of Marilyn's love for her

Mother, Marilyn was able to help her Mother financially in the earliest stages of her career.

A group of 42 receipts exists, ranging in date from October 1962 through April 1966, addressed to Inez C. Melson, for the care of Monroe's mother, Gladys P. Eley, while she was staying at Rockhaven Sanitarium in Verdugo City, California. Included with the Rockhaven Sanitarium receipts are other invoices for products and services provided to Eley, including prescription medications, toothbrushes and toothpaste, repairs to her dentures, cash advances, and package deliveries sent to Gainsborough, Florida, for Eley's other daughter, Berniece Miracle, (Marilyn's half-sister). April 27, 1966, invoice indicates that Eley's account at Rockhaven was $7,355.90 in arrears.

Marilyn's Mother, Gladys Pearl Monroe, died on March 11, 1984, at age of 82,
(Twenty-one years after Marilyn died).

Marilyn's Mother **Gladys Pearl Monroe** placed little Norma Jeane in the care of Gladys neighbors, the Bolender family, Ida, and Wayne, who fostered Norma Jeane at only two weeks old. Gladys was both financially and mentally incapable of raising her daughter. The religious, church-going foster family, with children of their own, wanted to adopt Norma Jeane. Fortunately, Gladys was able to get her mental capacity back once again to take care of Marilyn.

"Sadly, within just a few months after regaining custody of Marilyn, Gladys had a major breakdown and was "diagnosed as a paranoid schizophrenic. She spent the rest of her life going in and out of mental hospitals;" however, both Gladys and Marilyn never stopped corresponding. They continued their Mother/Daughter's love throughout their lives."

After Marilyn made it big in Hollywood, in the 1950s, we understand she paid a woman to monitor her Mother's progress.

Marilyn's Grandmother – Dellamae Hogan Monroe died in August 1927, at age 51, in Norwalk (now Metropolitan) State Hospital, where she was treated for *"manic depressive psychosis."*

Marilyn's Grandfather, Otis Elmer Monroe, a painter by trade, married Della Mae Hogan and had three children. He passed away in July 1909 in Patton State Hospital, San Bernardino, California, the USA, with a diagnosis of *"general paresis."*

Marilyn's maternal half-brother (from Gladys's first marriage) **Robert Kermitt Baker**, was born in January 1918, died on August 16, 1933, at age 15.

From **Berniece's (Marilyn's half-sister)** book, "My Sister Marilyn" A Memoir of Marilyn Monroe, *"... Robert was just an unlucky child. At about the age of three, he fell out of a car while his parents were arguing, and because of the accident, he walked with a limp. He was diagnosed with tuberculosis of his bone, and his kidneys failed eventually as a teenage boy..."*

Marilyn's maternal half-sister (from Gladys's first marriage) **Bernice Baker Miracle**, was born in July 1919, Los Angeles, CA. She is 100 years old in 2019 and still alive as of this writing. Bernice was the only female sibling to the Asphalt Jungle (1950) actress. They met only a half-dozen times. After the death of Marilyn Monroe, Marilyn left her sister Bernice $10,000.

Marilyn's niece – **Mona Rae Miracle** 80 years old (daughter of Bernice and Paris Miracle) Mona loved her Aunt Marilyn, and Marilyn had the same feelings for her. Marilyn taught her niece when she was only five years old not to stand straight while being photographed; she said, according to Mona: *"Tilt your head to the side, make a silly smile. Bend one knee, so you look a little curvy."*

Marilyn Monroe speaks - I'm Not an Orphan!

Question; regarding your Mother, do you see her as just a woman with white hair?

Marilyn's words: *"...Um actually she was when I was I was very young um I called every woman I would see, I'd say oh there's a momma, and if I would see a man, I'd say there's a daddy or papa I guess you say in French, so to learn that she was my Mother it was quite a shock you know, it was the woman with the red hair. The people I was staying with, I was about three (foster parents Albert and Ida Bolender) and um one morning I was having a bath actually and uh I referred to the woman as momma and she said "I'm not your mother "the one who comes here with the red hair and she said "don't call me Mother anymore, call me Aunt so on and so on. But the one I was concerned about was her husband, I say, "but he's my daddy" and she said, no you call him uncle. I know they weren't my aunt and uncle. I never lived with my mother, and I don't know about the 12 days old. I don't remember, but I know I was very young. I used to ask where my Mother was, oh I don't know I was about when I was put in the orphans home, and I refused to go into the orphans home, I mean I said I saw the orphan I could read at ten, and I put my feet down on the sidewalk they had to drag me in because I'm not an orphan..."*

Marilyn's words, *"...Counting the orphans home, I'll try, let's see, some places I was taken there at the end of the school term, and they were planning to keep me, but then after the summer, they'd had enough (laughter), so um for whatever reason, and then I was taken to another place, so there's one of so many. I know I went to six different grammar schools, you know, that's before uh uh you're in the seventh grade, but, I'll try to recall, let's see, I'm to nine, so for, just a second, ten, ten but I moved back to a place where I had stayed, so that makes eleven different moves, but ten, ten counting the orphans home."*

Looking out of the window of Marilyn's orphanage dormitory, which she shared with 26 other girls, looked out upon the former RKO Studio's water tower and led to her dreams of someday becoming a world-famous movie star. Seriously an all-time favorite inspirational quote of Marilyn's reads, *"I used to think as I looked at the Hollywood night, 'There must be thousands of girls sitting alone like me, dreaming of becoming a movie star. But I'm not going to worry about them. I'm dreaming the hardest."*

Grace used to come to the orphanage and take me out sometimes my Mother's best friend I could put on her lipstick she would take me someplace to have my hair curled, things like that meant a great deal to me. I cleaned the dormitory where id slept everything had t be perfect, you swept, and you dusted we had a bed a chair, a locker downstairs. We had to earn money there, I washed one hundred plates, a hundred cups, spoons, and forks, and you make five dents a month, and they took one penny for Sunday school, so you had one penny left so you hoped you could buy your friend some little thing at Christmas. I complained bitterly to grace my guardian, and there were these people who took me for a while, Grace was financially unable to care for me, but, I am very grateful that they at least assumed the responsibility because I could've just been kept there until I'm eighteen.

Marilyn also said, *"... I used to spend the whole afternoon trying to fit my foot into prints that were too big, and I would get down and measure my hands, and the prints were very large, I always had small hands and feet, so I became very discouraged at an early age..."*

Marilyn Monroe talks about Stuttering

Marilyn talks; *"First time was at the orphanage, and then later in my teens I stuttered, and I was um ah they elected me secretary of the English class, no, secretary of the minutes English class whatever you call, and ah then I say minutes of the last meeting, then I go mmm mm mmm (laughter) oh it's terrible. When? I don't know, I'd say at the orphanage, and after I left I guess and then when I was about thirteen, I took it up again (laughter) it just, I don't know uh how it happened, I just stuttered. Sometimes if I was very nervous or excited, in fact, one time I had a small part in a movie and uh assistant director came and yelled at me, oh he talked awful, and he rrr rr rrr so when I got into the scene, instead of my lines I go woo woo woo and my director came over to me and says, you don't stutter, and I said that's what you think! (Laughter) Oh, it's painful Oh God!"*

Rare 1964 Interview with Norma Jeane's Foster Parents

"...Norma Jeane was born in a maternity ward of the LA County Hospital. Norma Jeane was taken twelve days later to Hawthorne CA there; she was placed in the hands of Ida Bolender, who, along with her husband, would act as foster parents for seven to eight years. At ten months,

violence shook the baby's world when her grandmother Della Monroe went berserk. She came to the Bolenders one day for no reason, and she broke in the front door, and we (the Bolendeners) called the police. The Bolendeners look back on the hard years, and boarding children helped earn a living. We went to Sunday school with her lots of time I had not only her and my son I had other children too with me I could always go and handle four or five children to church, but they went to Sunday school if they were able. Marilyn Monroe lived in a mirage of relationships, thirteen foster brothers and sisters came and went grown-ups appeared and disappeared. It was hard to know what was real..."

Marilyn's words, at recess during elementary school "... I lived to play- I had to pretend things like all the kids we played real dramas excessive adventures..."

"I loved to invent – think more than the others – because, at my foster parent's home, everything was so predictable," Joy had been a random thing for Marilyn's Mother, the young film laboratory worker. Gladys Bakers' first two children, taken by her former husband. Although she paid 25.00 a month for Marilyn's care, Gladys occasionally visited Norma Jeane during weekends and took the child on outings, (Photographs exist of Gladys taking Norma Jeane to Santa Monica beach outings with friends, as a toddler at three years old (1929)

Norma Jeane went to live with her mother, who managed to make a down payment on a house near the Hollywood bowl. A beautiful white baby grand piano was the most prized furnishing that Marilyn cherished – after Marilyn's Mother was institutionalized, the piano was sold, after years of searching, Marilyn finally located the piano and regained possession of this sentimental attachment with her baby grand piano. As of 2019, the piano is now in possession of singer Mariah Carey.

Marilyn words (after her Mother's institutionalization) -"...*We only had the home for about, oh, I don't even think it was three months because she was taken away, my Mother.*"

At this point in Marilyn's life, we've come to realize there's possibly potential mental illness that runs in Marilyn Monroe's family.

Was Marilyn Monroe Mentally Ill?

As you've read through the previous chapters in our book, there is no definitive answer or conclusion that Marilyn Monroe was mentally ill. As we previously identified, we believe that Marilyn Monroe had a substance abuse or use problem. This potential problem, Marilyn Monroe, had most likely masked a perceived mental illness. How do we know this? We don't; however, during Marilyn Monroe's lifetime, the DSM-I was the manual to diagnosis mental illness. There is no confirmation that we could find that relates to a definitive answer from any of her psychiatrist, phycologist, or doctors that document a mental illness with a classification from the DSM-I. Now we have clinicians who can make a Dual Diagnosis, which includes Mental Illness and Substance Abuse – however, in most cases, the substance abuse problem 'should' be corrected before the mental illness problem would repair - Fact or Fiction!

It is important to realize that during Marilyn's most formative years, ages one-seven, and after that, there was no diagnosis of mental illness of any kind during Marilyn Monroe's younger years.

By now, wouldn't you think that a child who's been through so much amount of trauma that they would show signs of disturbance? Marilyn Monroe highly challenged with much chaos during her youth; however, this is proof that this now grown woman favorably demonstrated the power of her inner strength; this reminds me of a famous quote, *"That which does not kill us makes us stronger."* By Friedrich Nietzsche. I get the feeling deep down Marilyn knew that one day, if she worked hard at something that it would pay off and was possibly thinking she had to work like she had no money …that's called very powerful determination.

ATTACHMENTS

Marilyn's first home she ever purchased at 12305 5th Helena Drive Brentwood CA. On August 4, 1962, Marilyn spent her day at home, poolside, with her dog "Maf." Pat Newcomb was her guest that day. Eunice Murray was dropped off at Marilyn's in the morning. Marilyn was looking forward to a delivery from Frank's nursery. An order she had placed on August 1, 1962

PHONE
EXbrook
4-5262

FRANKS
NURSERIES AND FLOWERS
12424 WILSHIRE BOULEVARD

PHONE
GRanite
3-3336
3-6633

WEST LOS ANGELES 25, CALIF., 5—1— 19 62

DELIVER TO Miss Marilyn Monroe
ADDRESS 1230 — 5th Helena Dr.

CHARGE TO
ADDRESS

CHG.	CLERK	PHONE	SUN.	MON.	TUES.	WED.	THURS.	FRI.	SAT.	A.M.	P.M.	C.O.D.
2	Pak Plumosa								1 25	2 50
3	6" Cedrum Confusum								1 95	5 85
1	Flat Petunias								4 00	4 00
2	flat Tomatos								49	98
3	flats Begonias								49	1 47
1	Flat Blue Grass sod								4 00	4 00
1	Bx Tomatos								65	65
2	4" Begonias								59	1 18
4	18" Terra Cotta								8 95	35 80
3	Hummingbird feeder								1 00	3 00
3	pkg " food								39	1 17
										60 60
										2 43
	Thank You									63 02
	THIS IS A CONFIRMATION OF YOUR ORDER 2 flats									63 53

3337-40

No claims for adjustment will be made unless filed within 24 hours after delivery and must be accompanied with sales slip. No warranty is given as to productiveness of any seeds, bulbs or plants.

Eunice Murray at Marilyn home in front of some nursery items from Frank's nursery A Marilyn Monroe receipt for plants, 1962

"A beige carbon copy from 'Frank's Nurseries and Flowers' on Wilshire Boulevard in West Los Angeles; a sales clerk's handwritten notations read in part "8-1-62 / Miss Marilyn Monroe / 12305 5th Helena Dr of(f) Carmelina" and continues with items ordered including "tuberosa Orange king, bougainvillea hanging Begonia, Mexican lime" and "Valencia orange" among a few other misspelled flowers totaling "$93.08;" additional note on bottom reads "ask for Mr. Jeffrey;" 'Jeffrey' being Norman Jefferies (Eunice Murray's son-in-law and MM's handyman) who was at Monroe's house on the last day of her life, probably watering these plants she would never enjoy as she died just four days after this receipt was issued."

Marilyn Monroe's first home purchased in early 1962 at 12305 5th Helena Drive Brentwood, CA

A tranquil place for her to escape from the pressures of fame-

Marilyn had these Spanish styled wooden unique entry gates especially made for her new home

Marilyn's much interest in Spanish Décor

Entry tile "My Journey Ends Here."

CHAPTER 11

The Continued Fascination of Marilyn

At nine years old, Marilyn Monroe was taken to the Los Angeles Orphans Home Society (now Hollygrove) in September 1935. In 1937, when Norma Jeane was eleven years old, Marilyn's life at this point began to stabilize. Why? Gladys was close friends with her co-worker Grace Goddard, at the RKO studios. Grace remarked she seen stardom with Norma Jeane; Grace Goddard's Aunt was known as Aunt Ana to Marilyn whom Marilyn grew very fond of, Marilyn loved Aunt Ana Lower deeply. Aunt Ana played a major role part in Marilyn's up-bringing during the tender age of eleven-twelve when Aunt Ana helped raise her, with the permission of her guardian Grace McKee Goddard and remained at Aunt Ana's until her first marriage. Marilyn later said that Ana was the first person she ever really loved, and who loved her back. This kindhearted letter from Aunt Ana demonstrates the close bond between them;

"October 10, 1944
My precious Girl
You are outward bound on a Happy Journey,
May each moment of its joyous expectations
Be filled to the Brim.
New places, faces and
Experiences await you.
You will meet these all with your usual sweetness
and loving courtesy.

When you see your Sister
You will truly both receive a blessing.
Give her my love and a kiss, also
the dear little daughter,
My love also to the fortunate father and husband.
My happiness is much that
You are to have a needed rest
And lovely visit with your dear ones
Give Bibi a kiss for me too
One joy of going away is the

Coming back, where all who love you
(and who does not?)
Will be waiting with open arms to receive you
My Prayer will be –
Dear Father Keep thou, my child
On upward swing
Tonight, and Always
The following Lines will help you
Know your protection at all times
"I know that where I am
Is God. Since this is so.
No place can safer be than where I go."

Good night dearest
With Love and Kisses
Aunt Ana"

While Marilyn's youthful memories were bittersweet, she had nothing but praise for Ana. It appears the churchgoing Bolenders and Aunt Ana's faith contributed to Marilyn's foundation in her faith and strength.

Aunt Ana's teachings were seldom far from Marilyn's mind, and Maurice Zolotow (a show business biographer), *"has suggested that it was because of her influence that Marilyn was able to develop the imaginative skills she needed in her chosen profession, and to cope with the harsh realities of life."*

It was the most stable home environment that Marilyn had known, and she lived here until Aunt Ana Lower developed health problems. Therefore, Grace Goddard arranged a marriage between 16-year-old Norma Jeane and 21-year-old Jim Dougherty.

Andre De Dienes, one of the first photographers to work with Norma Jeane, wrote of a discussion they had during a modeling assignment in 1945. *"I was reading to her from a quotation book I had brought along with quotations about most everything that touches spiritual life. Norma Jeane listened attentively, and then she took from her handbag her Christian Science prayer book, and she, too, read for me."*

Norma Jeanes First Husband

Jim Dougherty, Married from June 1942 - September 1946 – In 1942, Mr. Goddard took a job in West Virginia and decided that Norma Jeane would not move with them. Grace did not want her placed in yet another orphanage or foster home, so she had come up with a plan to marry off Norma Jeane, with the boy next door, 21-year-old James Dougherty. Jim had genuine feelings for Norma Jeane, and he did not hesitate to ask her to marry him. Norma Jeane liked Jim as well and went along with it and became Mrs. James Dougherty less than three weeks after her sixteenth birthday, on June 19, 1942.

World War II was raging, and men were going away to fight, and the roles of the women they left behind were changing. In the case of Norma Jeane, it would be a change in a way that no one who knew her in her childhood could ever have expected.

This would be the beginning of Norma Jeane Mortenson's childhood, to her young womanhood, a journey to becoming Marilyn Monroe. Gladys, Marilyn's Mother, did not approve of her Hollywood life.

Card to Miss Norma Jeane Dougherty from Her Mother

"Dear One, I am very grateful for all the kindness you've shown me, and as a Loving Christian Scientist (my pencil broke), I hope our God will let me return some goodness to you without doing myself any harm. For I know good is reflected in goodness, the same as Love is reflected in Love./ As a Christian Scientist, I remain very truly your Mother." The undated note is in an un-postmarked envelope addressed to "Miss Norma Jeane Dougherty 6707 Odessa Ave., Van Nuys Cal." with a return address for her mother listed as "From - G. P. Eley 2713 Honolulu Ave. Verdugo City, Cal."

Head of 20th Century Fox Ben Lyon discusses how Norma Jeane became Marilyn Monroe, he stated:

"My secretary rang and said Mr. Lyon there's a very beautiful young girl here to see you, but she doesn't have an appointment, I said well you don't have to have an appointment to see me, send her in. So, a moment later, walked in the most gorgeous young girl you've ever seen in your life! She had golden hair, a beautiful dress, and only twenty-two years old. And I said sit down, so she sat by the desk, and I'd begun asking her various questions; what she'd done, she told me a little extra work and a bit here and there, and I said what your ambition is? She said to be a film star, and I looked at her, and I said honey you're in pictures and I think you will be a film star.

I said to her one day, Marilyn, why do you work so hard? The other kids that are under contract I sometimes call around eleven, twelve o'clock; they're still steeping from being out the night before. I don't think you can use Norma Jeane Doherty; if you're going to be a star, we've got to change your name; by the contract, we have a right to change the name. So, she agreed, and we looked in the books and thought about all kinds of combinations of names, nothing suited us, and finally, I remembered a girl I knew in New York a stage star, by the name of Marilyn Miller and I said to me, you're a Marilyn, and she said that's a lovely name, I said alright, that's your first name. We couldn't find a second name, she suddenly turned to me and said Mr. Lyon, can I use my grandmother's name? I said, what was that? She said Monroe, "Marilyn Monroe." Marilyn would take dramatic lessons for three hours, then have lunch, then dancing lessons for an hour, singing lessons for an hour, fencing lessons for an hour and then go on the backlot and ride, horseback."

Marilyn's words, *"...well, Mr. Lyon, I work hard because one day, maybe an opportunity will knock, and I want to be prepared..."* ***(Norma Jeane Doherty changed her name to Marilyn Monroe in August of 1946. She legally changes it on February 23, 1956.)***

Joe DiMaggio, Married from January 1954 - October 1954

In 1952, Marilyn began dating Joe DiMaggio; they lived at 2393 Castilian Drive L.A., Marilyn was living here with Joe, while Joe was still married to his previous wife. The home was also Spanish style, similar to the only home Marilyn ever purchased at 12305 5th Helena Drive. Brentwood CA.

Joe was the son of Italian immigrant parents, and he grew up in San Francisco, CA, with his four brothers and four sisters.

DiMaggio is an All- American New Your Yankees slugger who asked an acquaintance to arrange a dinner date with Monroe. They began dating, preferring to keep a low profile. Joe asks Marilyn to marry him several times. They married at San Francisco City Hall. They spent their first day of honeymoon at the Clifton Motel in Paseo Robles, CA. They spend two weeks in a house near Idyllwild, in a house owned by Marilyn's lawyer. During their short term marriage in 1954, Marilyn was learning to cook here, as they had many family and friends over for meals. Marilyn received great news from Fox during this time to come back on the set of "Pink Tights." Marilyn didn't show up on the set for "Pink Tights," therefore - suspended. Joe had always tried to protect Marilyn from the corruption of the studios' executives; Joe finally succeeded somewhat protecting Marilyn from deviant people.

In 1954, Marilyn displayed her gratitude for our troops by taking time away from her honeymoon in Tokyo with Joe DiMaggio to visit troops in Korea. Joe DiMaggio talks about Marilyn in japan. *"Well, everything has been fine. We've enjoyed our trip, the only thing that I have to complain about is I haven't seen very much of Marilyn…She was making a trip to Korea, touring through the camps, and so maybe after that, we'll be able to spend a little time together."* It was a huge hit featuring her onstage sparkling purple dress! Performing ten shows, for over four days to more than 100,000 soldiers and marines in 1954, who were celebrating the end of three years of combat? Photos continue to surface from some of the troops who were lucky enough to see Marilyn perform as she was mingling and laughing with troops and signing autographs, looking completely comfortable with the attention; this was one of the biggest highlights of Marilyn's life.

Marilyn's sparkling purple gown and matching bolero jacket, owned by a private collector in Australia, is quite stunning. This particular dress hasn't been seen by the public in over twenty years, until recently as it surfaced at the "Marilyn Monroe exhibit in Bendigo, Australia. It continues to sparkle as she did back in 1954, as Marilyn sang, *"Diamonds are a girl's best friend."*

It was during the filming of "The Seven Year Itch" in 1954, the couple got into a huge argument over her famous blowing skirt scene. They would divorce later that year.

No sooner the movie "There's No Business Like Show Business" wrapped, Marilyn was ushered immediately, without a break to rest, rushed to the set of "The Seven Year Itch" Joe had become completely fed up with the Hollywood scene and how Marilyn was being mistreated by the studios, taking a toll on their marriage. Marilyn had collapsed three times during the production of "Show Business" weather from marital problems or lack of rest. It was the famous skirt blowing up over a subway grate scene at 52nd and Lexington Avenue in New Your City that delighted a crowd of more than 2,000 onlookers. Marilyn paid a high price for becoming a movie star, and Joe felt this legionary scene was exposing too much of Marilyn's skin. Could it be Joe was protecting Marilyn from the movie industry, and the pressure it can bring on an induvial, or was Joe simply a jealous man? Their marriage only lasted nine months; however, they continued to remain closed after the split. Joe comments, *"No man ever satisfied her as I did."* Joe had one son from his first marriage. Joe's son was very close to Marilyn, and it's said to be Joe Paul DiMaggio III's happiest days that may have been in the company of his step Mother, Marilyn Monroe. Joe DiMaggio and his son were deeply crushed over the news of Marilyn's death. Joe excluded several of Marilyn's friends, including the Kennedy brothers. Joe believed that Robert and John Kennedy were involved in the murder of Marilyn. For twenty years, Joe used to send roses from the well-known Parisian Florist to Marilyn Monroe's gravesite. He loved her dearly.

DiMaggio's dedication to Monroe, even after their divorce, is well known, and love letters bring that longing into focus;

"I love you and want to be with you… There is nothing I would like better than to restore your confidence in me," Joe DiMaggio wrote to Marilyn Monroe

Marilyn's second husband, Joe DiMaggio, opens up his heart about the pain he felt on finding out Marilyn was filing for divorce after seeing her announcement on TV.

After writing about how much he loves her, he ends his letter with a handwritten note saying, *"I will go mad here. I love you!"*

With her marriage to DiMaggio, lasting less than a year, being single and interested in Miller. Marilyn even forged a relationship with his friends Norman and Hedda Rosten to get closer to the playwright.

Arthur Miller from June 1956 - January 1961

Marilyn Monroe's third marriage to Arthur Miller, even though they were opposites: movie star sex symbol in love and a cerebral, award-winning playwright communist. But in the end, Miller, just like her second spouse, Joe DiMaggio, wasn't enough for the fragile actress, feelings of inner discontentment and frustration began to surface. Also, to marital stressors, failed pregnancies, misunderstandings, and clashes overwork, Marilyn's continuous challenges contributed to her drinking and drug use, proving impossibilities.

Marilyn first encountered Miller in 1950, and at the time, she was trying to find fame while he was acclaimed as one of the country's leading playwrights.

Was Arthur a questionable influence for Marilyn?

As much as Arthur loved Marilyn, the influence of Arthur's deep involvement in communism affected Marilyn from the things she learned from Arthur and his communist pack. When Miller, instructed by Kazan, took Marilyn to a party, he didn't act on his obvious attraction to her. Marilyn believed this indicated his disrespect for her, which was more than enough to make him stand out from other men she knew. She told a friend of the encounter, *"It was like running into a tree, you know, like a cool drink when you've had a fever."*

Marilyn saw Miller off at the airport in January 1951 when he returned to New York. He'd told her how unhappy his current marriage was, so she expected he'd soon return. In the meantime, she placed his photo on a bookshelf above her pillow. But though the two exchanged letters, the pair reunited four years after their first encounter and began an affair.

Marilyn and Miller didn't meet again in person until 1955 after she'd moved to New York City to study at the Actors' Studio.

According to Wikipedia: After filming for The Seven Year Itch wrapped up in November 1954, Marilyn left Hollywood for the East Coast, New York, in late 1954; it was shortly after where she and Milton Greene met. Milton Greene is an American fashion and celebrity photographer and film and television producer where the two founded their own production company, Marilyn Monroe Productions (MMP)

A new adventure for Marilyn during this year, yet Marilyn, was very comfortable and becoming dedicated to bettering her acting career. When going out in New York, Marilyn was flamboyant with discretion -regardless of being dressed up or dressed or down, makeup or no makeup. Her lips could defiantly draw anyone's attention, her warm charisma and sexy persona attracted crowds from both male and female.

Marilyn became introduced to Lee Strasberg in early 1955;

Lee became Marilyn's mentor and teacher. Marilyn also bonded with Paula, his wife, who also coached Marilyn, Marilyn came to rely heavily on Lee for her professional development; she frequently attended sessions at the Actors Studio.

"Fox awarded her a new contract in late 1955, which increased her salary. Her roles included an acclaimed performance in Bus Stop (1956) and her first independent production, The Prince and the Showgirl (1957). Monroe won a Golden Globe for Best Actress for her work in Some Like It Hot (1959), a critical and commercial success. Her last completed film was the drama The Misfits (1961)."

Marilyn Monroe deeply personal letter to Paula Strasberg

A single page of lined yellow notebook paper folded multiple times and addressed on the exterior of the folded page "To Paula/ Personal MM." *The letter reads "Paula Dear,/ You asked me yesterday why-/ I felt somehow (I'm only conceiving of it this morning) that if I didn't have the control or the will to make myself do anything simple & do it right, I would never be able to act or do anything - I know it sounds crazy - maybe it was even superstitious - I don't know - I don't know anything./ Something has happened, I think, to make me lose my confidence. I don't know what it is. All I know is I want to work./ Oh, Paula, I wish I knew why I am so anguished. I think maybe I'm crazy like all the other members of my family were; when I was sick I was sure I was. I'm so glad you are with me here!"*

Marilyn Monroe's Handwritten Prose New York in 1955

With multiple verses in pencil and ink on front and back of page - The primary verse on recto was written as Marilyn observed Manhattan from her suite at the hotel, reading in part, *"Sooooo many lights in the darkness/ making skeletons of buildings/ and life in the streets."* A poem about trees that appears to begin in the upper left margin of recto and continues onto the lower right of verso reads in full, *"Sad, sweet trees-/ I wish for you-rest/ but you must be wakeful/ You must suffer-/ to loose [sic] your dark golden/ when your covering of/ even dead leaves leave you/ strong and naked/ you must be-/ alive-when looking dead/ straight though bend/ with wind/ And bear the pain & the joy/ of newness on your limbs."*

Strasberg's an important and influential presence in Marilyn's life so much that she made the Strasberg's the major beneficiaries of her will.

Coincidently the Strasberg's address was shared with MaryAnn Kris, who was Marilyn's psychiatrist in New York

It was Kris who committed Marilyn to the New York's Payne Whitney Psychiatric Clinic.

A vintage file copy of a six-page typed letter from Monroe to Dr. Ralph Greenson, the California-based psychiatrist who treated Monroe in the period leading up to her death. This deeply emotional letter, dated March 2, 1961, was written while Monroe was staying at Columbia Presbyterian Medical Center for three weeks of recuperation following her stay at New York's Payne Whitney Psychiatric Clinic. Passages in the letter include:

"There was no empathy at Payne-Whitney — it had a very bad effect — they asked me after putting me in a 'cell' (I mean cement blocks and all) for very disturbed depressed patients (except I felt I was in some kind of prison for a crime I hadn't committed. The inhumanity there, I found archaic. They asked me why I wasn't happy there (everything was under lock and key; things like electric lights, dresser drawers, bathrooms, closets, bars concealed on the windows — the doors have windows so patients can be visible all the time; also, the violence and markings still remain on the walls from former patients). I answered: 'Well, I'd have to be nuts if I like it here.'"

"I sat on the bed trying to figure if I was given this situation in an acting improvisation what would I do. So I figured, it's a squeaky wheel that gets the grease. I admit it was a loud squeak, but I got the idea from a movie I made once called Don't Bother to Knock. I picked up a light-weight chair and slammed it, and it was hard to do because I had never broken anything in my life — against the glass intentionally. It took a lot of banging to get even a small piece of glass – so I went over with the glass concealed in my hand and sat quietly on the bed waiting for them to come in. They did, and I said to them 'If you are going to treat me like a nut I'll act like a nut.' I admit the next thing is corny but I really did it in the movie except it was with a razor blade. I indicated if they didn't let me out, I would harm myself — the furthest thing from my mind at that moment since you know Dr. Greenson, I'm an actress and would never intentionally mark or mar myself. I'm just that vain."

The letter also takes several sentimental turns with Monroe fondly referencing Joe DiMaggio and Yves Montand. Marilyn closed the letter with *"I think I had better stop because you have other things to do but thanks for listening for a while. Marilyn M."*

Sometimes all people want to do is sleep, to heal! It seems Marilyn was overworked and just needed to rest.

Soon Miller and Monroe embarked upon an affair, although he remained a married man. However, in the years since they'd first met, she'd become a star - This meant the press paid close attention to every move Monroe made, and their affair couldn't remain a secret.

Marilyn wanted to be with Miller, who seemed to offer her both love and the sense of security she'd always yearned for. She also liked the idea of being seen as a serious actress partnered with a renowned playwright. Miller was reluctant to leave his wife, but he was very much in love with Monroe; in one letter, he told her, *"I believe that I should die if I ever lost you."* In the spring of 1956, he went to Nevada to establish residency so he could divorce his wife.

Monroe was counseled to distance herself from Miller or possibly see her career go up in smoke. However, she ignored this advice, remaining loyal to Miller both publicly and privately. Her devotion was a benefit for Miller, as it was hard to get the public to turn against a man who'd won the heart of an American goddess.

Miller and Monroe married in 1956 but had problems immediately

Though Miller was cited for contempt (his subsequent conviction would eventually be overturned on appeal), he did get his passport. Miller and Monroe got married on June 29, 1956, in a judge's office in White Plains, New York; a Jewish ceremony followed on July 1. Together, they next headed to England so Monroe could work on "The Prince and the Showgirl" with Laurence Olivier.

Marilyn was delighted by her marriage, saying at one point, *"...this is the first time I've been really in love..."* But the movie shoot didn't go smoothly, and she clashed with Olivier. Then she happened upon notes Miller had been making about her. The exact words she read are unknown, but they related that Miller was disappointed by their marriage and sometimes found Monroe embarrassing.

Monroe told Lee and Paula Strasberg about what Miller had written. *"How he thought I was some angel, but now he guessed he was wrong. That his first wife had let him down, but I had done something worse."* She idealized Miller and was devastated by what she viewed as a betrayal.

Adding to the stress of the marriage, Monroe suffered several miscarriages

Monroe's discovery in England wasn't enough to end her marriage. She and Miller would have happy moments, such as when he dedicated an edition of his collected plays to her. Monroe also tried to embrace a quieter life of cooking and homemaking. But these moments of happiness were interrupted by other problems.

Marilyn was particularly devastated by her inability to give birth to Miller's child. She experienced a miscarriage in September 1956, lost an ectopic pregnancy in August 1957, and had a second miscarriage in December 1958, shortly after she'd finished shooting *"Some Like It Hot."* A regular user and abuser of pills and alcohol, Marilyn blamed herself for the last miscarriage.

She didn't like that he'd ignored his principles and did a lackluster rewrite of scenes for her film "Let's Make Love." And when she had an affair with co-star Yves Montand, she noted that Miller didn't fight for her, or even object to the liaison.

Their marriage ended after less than five years; this marriage and divorce may have been a contributing factor to Marilyn's vulnerability. *"All she ever wanted was to be loved."*

ATTACHMENTS

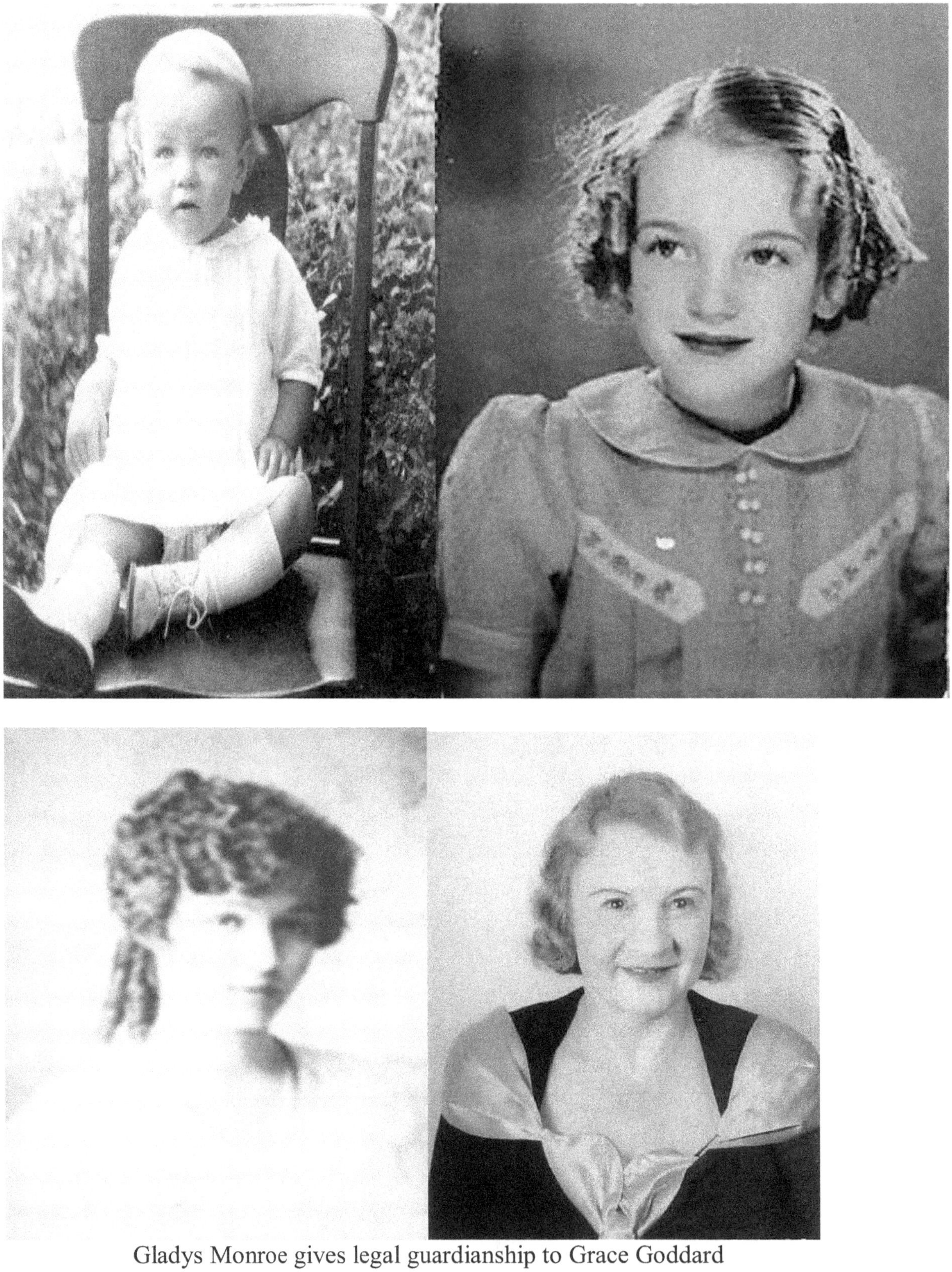

Gladys Monroe gives legal guardianship to Grace Goddard

Around nine years old, Norma Jeane was placed the Los Angeles Orphans Home Society (now "Hollygrove"). If you look real close, you can see the letters of her name written inside the name "Hollygrove."

This moment here was a very special moment for Marilyn; she held on to this, throughout her whole life. She looked out her window at the RKO window tower where her Mother worked. *"As the other kids slept and said, I used to think as I looked out on the Hollywood night, there must be thousands of girls sitting alone like me, dreaming of becoming a movie star. But I'm not going to worry about them.* **I'm dreaming the hardest.***"* She proved to herself…and so she did.

Gladys and baby Norma Jeane at the beach.
Gladys, with Norma Jeane as a teenager with Norma's half-sister Berniece Miracle Baker at the beach - looking so happy together. It's always a great day when we get to go to the beach. Marilyn spent much time at Southern California beaches during her life.

Marilyn's Grand Mother Della Mae, (Gladys' Mother). Her Husband was Otis Elmer Monroe. There are no portraits of Otis, but Della described him as light-skinned, red-haired, and brown-eyed. Della has a lot of hair, as Marilyn did.

Robert "Jackie" Baker, Marilyn's half-brother. I tend to think he resembles Marilyn.

Berniece Miracle Baker, Marilyn's half-sister…any resemblance in your opinion?

Marilyn's niece, Mona Rae Miracle, with Mother Berniece &. Marilyn with Berniece

Marion Otis Elmer Monroe. Gladys only sibling. Marilyn's Uncle. Died at age twenty-five

Martin Edward Mortensen father.

Marilyn always believed that Gifford was her

Which of Marilyn's three husbands do you believe was best for Marilyn?

Marilyn Monroe roams the studio backlot. Just 20 years old, she had impressed talent director Ben Lyon with her charm and innocence.

"I kept driving past the theater with my name on the marquee. 'Marilyn Monroe.' Was I excited? I wished they were using 'Norma Jeane' so that all the kids at home and schools who never noticed me could see it." Marilyn Monroe

Norma Jeane walked into Ben Lyon's office at Twentieth Century-Fox in July of 1946, unsure of her future but certain of her goals. Lyon interviewed her about her background and inquired about any training she might have had in show business. Lyon reportedly said of Norma Jeane Dougherty, "It's Jean Harlow all over again." Appointed executive talent director at Fox after the war, Lyon was adept at recognizing potential screen stars. He was less interested in the amount of acting talent that Norma Jeane possessed than in her charisma and unique charm, which he knew would be magnified on the screen. Norma Jeane had screen presence -- just as Harlow had -- and Lyon saw it.

Monroe in a studio publicity photo taken when she was a contract player at 20th Century-Fox in 1947. She appeared in two small film roles during the contract and was let go after a year

On February 23, 1956, Norma Jeane Mortenson changed her legal name to Marilyn Monroe (though she had been using it as a stage name for years). From a job at the Radioplane factory to the world-known sex bomb!

In a cold February in 1954, *Monroe said: "The trip was the best thing that ever happened to me. I never felt like a star before in my heart. It was so wonderful to look down and see a fellow smiling at me."*

God Bless our United States Military!

Marilyn Monroe's famous moment in history is wearing a white ivory halter cocktail dress in the 1955 film "The Seven Year Itch," directed by Billy Wilder. The dress created by costume designer William Travilla worn in one of the best-known scenes in the movie. The dress, regarded as an icon of film history, and the image of Monroe in the white dress standing above a subway grating blowing the dress-up described as one of the iconic images of the 20th century! (Sold for $4.6m in 2011).

Monroe Monroe's "Happy Birthday Mr. President" dress was made of a sheer and flesh-colored marquisette fabric, with 2,500 shimmering rhinestones sewn into it. The dress was so tight-fitting that Monroe had difficulty putting it on; this dress had to be sewn on to her figure, last minute; she wore nothing under it.

Monroe with U.S. Attorney General Robert F. Kennedy and President John F. Kennedy at the birthday celebration

President Kennedy's birthday celebration was held at the third Madison Square Garden on May 19, 1962, and more than 15,000 people attended, including numerous celebrities. The event was a fundraising gala for the Democratic Party. Marilyn's performance lasted approximately 30 seconds, but more than five decades later; it remains the most famous version of 'Happy Birthday' ever,"

Monroe sang the traditional "Happy Birthday to You" lyrics in a breathy, sultry, intimate voice, with "Mr. President" inserted as Kennedy's name. She continued the song with a snippet from the classic song, "Thanks for the Memory", for which she had written new lyrics specifically aimed at Kennedy.

Lyrics
"Happy Birthday to you,
Happy Birthday to you,
Happy Birthday Mr. President,
Happy Birthday to you.
Thank's Mr. President
For all the things you've done
The battles you've won
The way you deal with US Steel
And our problems by the ton,
We thank you, so much.
Everybody, Happy Birthday!'

Peter Lawford was at the event that night to introduce Monroe. He made a play on the actress's reputation for tardiness by giving her a number of introductions throughout the night, after which she did not appear on stage. When Monroe finally appeared in a spotlight, Lawford introduced her as the *"late Marilyn Monroe"*. Monroe peeled off her white ermine fur coat, revealing the dress, and the audience gasped.

Afterward, as an enormous birthday cake was presented to him, President Kennedy came on stage and joked about Monroe's version of the song, saying, *"I can now retire from politics after having had Happy Birthday sung to me in such a sweet, wholesome way,"* alluding to Marilyn's delivery, skintight dress, and image as a sex symbol.

The performance was one of her last major public appearances before her death less than three months later on August 4, 1962.

First Lady Jacqueline Kennedy, who rarely attended Democratic Party events, spent the day at the Loudon Hunt Horse Show with her children, John and Caroline. Regardless, why wasn't Jackie present with her family for her husband's Birthday Gala?

Julien's wrote in the release, *"The dress, the performance, Jacqueline Kennedy's absence and photographs from the evening would spark ravenous rumors of an affair between the president and Marilyn."*

Monroe's iconic dress was made by designer Jean Louis. This dress sold recently at a Los Angeles auction for $4.8 million and bought by museum chain Ripley's Believe It Or Not; this famous dress gratefully is on tour for many to enjoy its one of a kind beauty.

CHAPTER 12

Marilyn Monroe's Unique Character and Loving Spirit

Marilyn was perfect just the way she was born. However, to perfect her beauty, she was encouraged, in the 1950s, to undergo plastic surgery, so she did. A cartilage implant was placed in Marilyn's chin. A physician's notes on Marilyn Monroe reveal "that the Hollywood star had plastic surgery on her nose and chin... also a slight rhinoplasty."

Also, the information contained in medical notes and six X-rays of Marilyn Monroe's face was auctioned at Julien's in California in November 2013.

Also: records from Beverly Hills plastic surgeon Michael Gurdin appear to confirm that Monroe did have a chin implant, as has been speculated over the years. In his notes, Gurdin referred to a 1950 cartilage implant in Monroe's chin, which he wrote had begun to dissolve, a discovery he made after the actress complained of "a chin deformity."

Did her physical alterations honestly make Marilyn Monroe happy?

That moment at the Mocambo Marilyn help changed the life of Ella Fitzgerald

Mocambo in Hollywood During the '50s was one of the most popular venues in the area. Frank Sinatra frequented the Mocambo.

Because of her race, Ella was not allowed to sing at this establishment. Marilyn Monroe made a call that changed her life:

"I owe Marilyn Monroe a real debt... she personally called the owner of the Mocambo and told him she wanted me booked immediately, and if he would do it, she would take a front table

every night. She told him – and it was true, due to Marilyn's superstar status – that the press would go wild.

"The owner said yes, and Marilyn was there, front table, every night. The press went overboard. After that, I never had to play a small jazz club again. She was an unusual woman – a little ahead of her times. And she didn't know it."

Fitzgerald also had an influence on Marilyn. However, years before the Mocambo phone call, Monroe was studying the recordings of Fitzgerald. The continued study of Fitzgerald turned Marilyn into a relatively solid singer.

Some of the Things that brought Marilyn Monroe Happiness in Her Life - Animals - Marilyn enjoyed her fur babies

"...I like animals. If you talk to a dog or a cat, it doesn't tell you to shut up..." Marilyn Monroe *"....
Dogs never bite me, just humans..."*

Tippy was Marilyn's first dog. Given to Marilyn by her foster father, Al Bolender. (1930's)

Ruffles, and English Spaniel when Marilyn lived with the Godards (1940's)

Muggsie, a collie given to Norma Jeane by her first husband, James Doherty (late 1940's)

Josepha, a Chihuahua (late 1940's)

Hugo, a basset hound that lived with Marilyn and Arthur Miller in their New York Apartment, Arthur retained custody of Hugo. (Late 1950's)

Maf, a white poodle, a gift from Frank Sinatra, where Frank purchased the dog from Natalie Woods Mother. After Marilyn died in 1962, Maf, her poodle, was handed over to Frank Sinatra's secretary.

Marilyn boarded "Maf," a single-page invoice from the Southdown Kennel in Roxbury, Connecticut, dated December 18, 1961, for "Miss M. Munroe" for boarding and housebreaking of "Maf," Monroe's poodle. The charges include boarding between August 3 and December 14, 1961, at a rate of $75 per month for a total of $330, as well as brushings, shampoos, worming, and transportation to the airport for a total of $43 in additional charges.

Mitsou, a white Persian cat during the height of her career in New Your City (1950's)

Butch, a parakeet during her marriage with Arthur Miller

Ebony, a black horse Marilyn occasionally rode on the Connecticut farm she and Arthur Miller owned.

Marilyn worked with many animals during her career as an actress. She even didn't mind working with Ester, the chimpanzee, during the filming of "Monkey Business."

Marilyn's love for Children and Charity

Marilyn Monroe was truly a humanitarian. She had a big heart for helping people. Throughout her life, she is seen walking through children's hospitals, spreading cheer to young people. She toured and orphanage in Mexico shortly before her death, and donated money to help them. The World Adoption International Fund, The Arthritis and Rheumatism Foundation, The March of Dimes, The Milk Fund for Babies, St. Jude's Hospital, Toys for Tots. Marilyn kicked out the first ball at Ebbets Field for a charity soccer game between the US and Israel. Not to mention, Marilyn donated several days in Korea during her honeymoon, away from her then-husband, DiMaggio entertaining the troops, also spent time with soldiers at Camp Pendleton.

Being Marilyn didn't have any children of her own. She adored children and longed for a baby. She remained close to her stepchildren from her marriages, also spending time with child co-stars.

Reading gave Marilyn Solitude and Quest for Knowledge

Marilyn didn't have to read to be smart. Putting aside the books, she was intelligent, regardless of being a blonde. We see her beautiful library was filled with over 400 books! Her Literature reflected reading was one of her favorite hobbies. She enjoyed picking up a book for the mood, sitting by a window, or reading outdoors or in public. Marilyn indulged in books! A few books she had on her shelf were "How to Travel Incognito" "Thurber Country" "The Boston Cooking-School Cook Book" "From Russia with Love" "The Art of Loving" "The Last Temptation of Christ" "The Prophet" "On The Road" she also had books on writing …and the list goes on. It appears Marilyn had a broad mind for educating herself…Some of us love to read or talk about them. It's an exercise that challenges us to achieve more. It also allows us to experience and explores different places. Reading tends to relieve us from the constraints of our reality, taking us beyond our world into someone else's, whether real or imaginary. As a writer, I enjoy reading, to educate and progress on being informed, the benefit is, its relaxing, it places me on a journey into what I'm reading, taking our mind off the present moment. Some feel it helps the lonely and brings life. Reflecting on Marilyn's life, she was very passionate to better herself, grasping for a good read was a strengthening tool for her.

Marilyn is also famous for her inspirational quotes and her writings; some of Marilyn's most intimate soul-stirring thoughts are collected in Fragments; some of the favorite genres of books were poetry, classic literature, and politics. She was also a high school graduate.

"For life, it is rather a determination not to be overwhelmed. For work, the truth can only be recalled, never invented" **Marilyn Monroe**

"I'm finding that sincerity and to be simple or direct as (possible) id like is often taken for sheer stupidity, but since it is not a sincere world – it's very probable that being sincere is stupid. One probably is stupid to be sincere since it's in this world and no other world that we know for sure we exist – meaning that (since reality exists it should be met and dealt with) since there is the reality to deal with" **Marilyn Monroe**

"Stones on the walk/ every color there is/ I stare down at you/ like a horizon-/ the space-air is between us beckoning/, and I am many stories up/ my feet frightened/ as I grasp towards you."

Marilyn - Known for Jotting, Imaginative, Poetic Expressions about her Wants

Marilyn's jotting reveals a woman constantly striving to ground herself, help her, and keep on top of her terrors. They also show her determination and strong will: whether it is in the planning of dinner parties or the preparation of a performance, Marilyn was meticulous and dedicated to doing her best, always!

Her notebooks are often written in a scrappy, hurried hand, with crossings-out and annotations. In her so-called Record notebook from around 1955, she writes that her *"first desire was to be an actress"* and that she is striving to work fully and sensitively, *"without being ashamed of it."* Her drive to work on herself and her craft was merciless: *"I can and will help myself and work on things analytically no matter how painful,"* and she notes in her notebook a single line, *"having a sense of myself"* – as if the words ground her in some way and remind her of what she needs to keep in mind.

She writes, "I guess I have always been deeply terrified to really be someone's wife since I know from life one cannot love another, ever, really... starting tomorrow, I will take care of myself for that's all I really have, and as I see it now has ever had".

Marilyn Cooking Enjoyment

Marilyn didn't have to win her man's heart through her cooking? Being an avid reader, cookbooks were included in her book collection. Those of us who enjoy cooking are open to delicious dishes. Marilyn created her stuffing recipe, which is popular over the internet. She relished cooking and was conscious of her health and fitness…obviously. When married to James Doherty, she enjoyed making peas and carrots because she enjoyed the color combination, sound silly? But Marilyn was a beautiful kind of silly. Some accounts say Jimmie (James) said her dishes were horrendous, others say, she mastered the art of cooking game dishes. Will we ever know? Some photos imply.

Marilyn's protein-rich diet kept her in shape, especially because she occasionally treated herself to an ice cream sundae after attending evening drama classes. *"I'm sure I couldn't allow myself this indulgence was it not that my normal diet wasn't composed almost totally of protein foods."*

"Frankly, I've never considered my figure so exceptional; until quite recently, I seldom gave it any thought at all" (1952 Pageant Magazine – How I stay in shape)

"My biggest single concern used to be getting enough to eat."

While with Joe DiMaggio, Marilyn learned from one of Joe's sisters, she began to grill steaks, Matzah ball soup, fillet fish, and stuffed cabbage were some of her creations; even sourdough bread.

Marilyn Monroe's possession was also a softcover spiral-bound copy of Elena's Famous Mexican and Spanish Recipes, copyright 1944 Elena Zelayeta, 30th printing June 1, 1950, by Dettners Printing House, San Francisco. This best-selling cookbook by Zelayeta is credited with introducing traditional Mexican and Spanish cooking to many American households. I'm sure she enjoyed many authentic Mexican dishes during her frequent visits to Mexico.

She was a huge fan of her favorite champagne was Dom Perignon. A carbon copy receipt from the Jurgensen's grocery liquor department, Beverly Hills, listing order for 12 splits of Piper Heidsieck Champagne, for a total of $26.21. The receipt, dated December 2, 1959, lists a delivery date of "Thurs AM" to Marilyn Monroe at The Beverly Hills Hotel, Bungalow 21.

ATTACHMENTS

Because of her race, Ella Fitzgerald was not allowed to sing at this establishment. Marilyn Monroe made a call that changed her life:

"I owe Marilyn Monroe a real debt… she personally called the owner of the Mocambo and told him she wanted me booked immediately, and if he would do it, she would take a front table every night. She told him – and it was true, due to Marilyn's superstar status – that the press would go wild.

"The owner said yes, and Marilyn was there, front table, every night. The press went overboard. After that, I never had to play a small jazz club again. She was an unusual woman A little ahead of her times. And she didn't know it." – Ella Fitzgerald

Marilyn Monroe with "Maf"

Frank Sinatra gave Maf to Marilyn in 1961 while in New York. Marilyn would let Maf sleep on a white fur coat given to her by Arthur Miller. Maf was sent to Marilyn to live with her in Hollywood once she bought her house in Brentwood and intended to make it her permanent home.

"Dogs never bite me, just humans" Marilyn Monroe

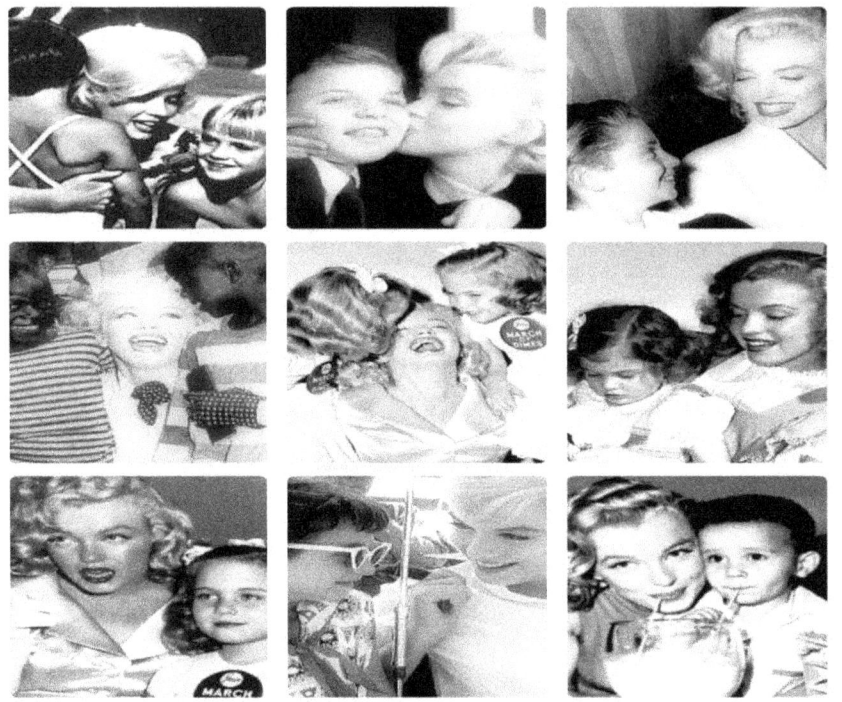

Marilyn always wanted children of her own. She loved children immensely on and off movie sets

Marilyn Monroe with co-star Eileen Heckart and her children on the set of "Bus Stop", 1956

Marilyn Monroe Santa Monica 1961   Norma Jeane Dougherty 1946

"And I loved the wind because it felt like it caressed me," Marilyn Monroe

CHAPTER 13

Marilyn Monroe, the Heartbeat of Hollywood's Legacy

Social Networking Seducing the World

Marilyn's sex appeal continues to fiercely capture her iconic personality, style, glamour, elegance, enduring a commanding presence on social media, with more than 8.3 million followers on Facebook pages and more than 183,000 followers on Twitter, to mention a few. Almost fifty-eight years after her death on August 4, 1962, Marilyn is more famous now than ever.

Who would have thought that Norma Jeane, from a suburb in Los Angeles, would later become the sexiest woman in the world; we all came to know and fell in love with more than the name of, Marilyn Monroe!

"…Imperfection is beauty, madness is genius, and it's better to be ridiculous than absolutely boring…" -Marilyn Monroe

Marilyn remains a huge success, her Estate, generating more than $30 Million in revenue annually.

When you search for "Marilyn Monroe," Google returns 64.4 Million hits about her. By comparison, Katharine Hepburn gets a measly 5 million, James Dean 34 million, and Frank Sinatra 43 million results. Elvis, on the other hand, is still the 'King' with close to 200 million search results. Why is Marilyn Monroe still a part of our lives - around the world, fifty- seven years later, in 2019? We see Marilyn everywhere in the public's eyes, with pictures on the walls in our home, clothing accessories, tattoos of Marilyn, perfume and jewelry…pretty much anything and everything we can think about. Even when we wake up with a cup of coffee with Marilyn's face on it, her beauty is a reflection of her persona. As the female author of this journal, when I wear anything with Marilyn's memorabilia, even wearing my Chanel No. 5, I feel 'pretty.' There's this sense of being carefree; she just makes you feel, good! A simple glance at her brings a sparkle to our eyes. Everyone has their subjective thoughts or feelings, making it hard to pinpoint what makes us individually drawn to her, yet we are. We believe that many people live vicariously through Marilyn Monroe - do you?

Let's take a walk with her fan stars of today who give an audience to Marilyn's look

From all ages and walks of life, through memory lane, to name a few, Michelle Williams, for portraying Marilyn Monroe in the drama "My Week with Marilyn" (2011), earning an Oscar nomination. Susan Sarandon played Marilyn Monroe's mother Gladys in a Lifetime movie, *"The Secret Life of Marilyn Monroe."*

Teen Choice Awards 2011, Taylor Swift channels Marilyn Monroe as she wears a halter dress as her skirt blows up. In which Marilyn stood atop a subway grate and let the breeze of a passing train as her skirt blew above her waist.

For "Marilyn's 86th birthday, Lady Gaga tweeted, *"Happy Birthday Marilyn - They'll never take our blonde hair and lipstick," along with a picture of herself, Monroe-like.* Nicki Minaj mentions she's "obsessed with Marilyn Monroe..."

Of course, Madonna, Grace Kelly, Nicole Kidman, who took a walk down memory lane to draw a strong comparison to Marilyn? Lindsay Lohan, Rihanna; Echoes Marilyn Monroe while shooting music videos for new song 'Pour It Up.'

Singers such as Christina Aguilera and Gwen Stefani. A show called "Smash" on NBC, follows a Broadway musical based on Marilyn's life, with two actresses competing for her part.

Thank you Sir! **Elton John song, "Candle in the Wind,"** who sang his hymn of "Candle in the Wind," it is a threnody with music and lyrics by Elton John and Bernie Taupin.

First written in 1973, in honor of Marilyn Monroe, who had died 11 years earlier. In 1997, Elton John performed a rewritten version of the song as a tribute to Diana, Princess of Wales.

His words still ring decades later. Marilyn's death remains one of Hollywood's most tantalizing mysteries –

Goodbye Norma Jean
Though I never knew you at all
You had the grace to hold yourself
While those around you crawled
They crawled out of the woodwork
And they whispered into your brain
They set you on the treadmill
And they made you change your name
And it seems to me you lived your life
Like a candle in the wind
Never knowing who to cling to
When the rain set in
And I would have liked to have known you
But I was just a kid
Your candle burned out long before
Your legend ever did
Loneliness was tough
The toughest role you ever played
Hollywood created a superstar
And pain was the price you paid
Even when you died
Oh the press still hounded you
All the papers had to say
Was that Marilyn was found in the nude
And it seems to me you lived your life
Like a candle in…

Banner, a professor of history and gender studies at the University of Southern California.

"She was extremely intelligent." But why has Marilyn's appeal only gotten stronger? "First of all, she died very young," says Banner, freezing her image for eternity. But another reason is the existence of thousands of photographs of Marilyn, bursting with life. "She's conceivably the most photographed person of the 20th century," "There are a lot of people making money off her,"

Kenneth Battelle was a leading New York hairdresser from the 1950s Marilyn's personal hairdresser from 1958-1962

Sometimes described as the world's first celebrity hairdresser, Kenneth achieved international fame for creating Jacqueline Kennedy's bouffant in 1961, arranged Marilyn Monroe for the famous JFK Birthday serenade. Unluckily, while the hairdresser was doing his thing, JFK was also doing his thing with both Jacqueline Kennedy and Marilyn Monroe.

An extremely rare lock of Marilyn Monroe's hair continues to captive fans around the world, sold for $10,177.

Gladys Rasmussen, Marilyn Monroe's Hair Stylist, 1952 Gladys said: *"Her hair is so curly naturally that to build a coiffure for her I have to first give her a straight permanent... The way we got her shade of platinum is with my own secret blend of sparkling silver bleach plus twenty-volume peroxide and a secret formula of silver platinum to take the yellow out".*

Allan Whitney Snyder Make-up Artist interviewed about Marilyn Monroe –

"You can talk your way into her get a lot of things from her just by giving a sad story, she gave a story of her own car a 1941 Pontiac when she wasn't making a lot of money, wasn't a star, inferior complex, she'd be there in time, shed play around, the worse thing was when she had to sing a song or something later on where she'd do nicely, she wasn't great, but a nice voice. She was a perfectionist acting-wise, that's the other reason these coaches got to her, and she worked with them so much because they thought she thought they could improve her so much and if she would've just been her cute little self she would've been so much better. Or, she could have right away had some children any child at least because she loved children so much, she went for children, puppies anything, had she had one of her own to take care of or a doll of her own to grow up with, I'm sure that would've helped her mentally. Once she started working, *some days she couldn't show up, she was sick. Finally, they dropped her, after about five or six weeks of off or on hit or miss situations of coming in the studio dropped her."*

One night, Marilyn was exhausted and said, *"Do you want to roll up my hair for me?"* She showed me how, but I didn't get it quite right. The rolls I made were smaller than her own usual ones.

We loved to talk about hair and clothes and makeup. Marilyn got a kick out of making up my face for me and showed me how to play down the darker shade to make cheeks look more hollow, or a lighter shade on a thin lip to make it look fuller. She was an artist with colors on her own face. She told me to be sure to make myself some little eyebrows — drawn on a little feather line down each temple where my eyebrows are sparse. She drew those on me and then did my eyes and my rouge and my lips, and after she finished, we went to the mirror and cracked up laughing at the stranger she had turned me into."

Zales The Diamond Store "Introducing 2019 "The Marilyn Monroe Collection" of Fine Jewelry Exclusively at Zales;

"I am a Diamond"
"Ï am my own Muse"
"The Diamonds are a girl's best friend store"

Dolce & Gabbana commercial Scarlett Johansson exposes Marilyn

"Oh I love Italy, I had an Italian boyfriend once, his Mother broke up with me, how do I know it was a lie, because I read it in your newspaper, well, a girl has to have a private life, keeps the public interested. Music inspires me. Art inspires me, but so does the wind, yes I can release it, but you'll have to pay me first uh my favorite part of my body - like my lips, for kissing and for words that start with the letter "M"

I do all my stunts, even the lovemaking, actress is the hardest because you never know who you are. I'm not an actress; I play one in the movies. Yes, I can cry like you...but the third take, that's for real. Um, the smell of sunshine the best, you know what I mean. I'm not looking for a million things, just that one perfect thing, 'Love.'"

The Statue

A 26-foot-tall, 34,000-pound statue of the Marilyn traversing the country: The famous seven-year itch white dress billowing and undies showing, now resting in Palm Springs, Calif

"Marilyn was the epitome of a certain kind of feminine ideal," says the co-author Nickens of "Marilyn in Fashion." Her key fashion legacy, he says, was to bring body-conscious clothes into everyday life, with elegance. Though she was not a fashion icon during her lifetime, Nickens thinks Marilyn shared something with other style icons like Jackie Kennedy, Grace Kelly, and Audrey Hepburn. "They didn't follow trends," he says. "It's about knowing yourself and what works for you, and having that confidence." Do you think Marilyn had confidence?

A Makeup Museum to Showcase Cosmetic Items from Marilyn Monroe, Greta Garbo.

-The museum, set to open in May 2020 in the Meatpacking District in New York-

Marilyn Monroe – Coco Channel and Brad Pitt

It's no secret that Marilyn Monroe was not a fan of the pajamas. The actress famously said in an interview in *1952 that she wore "...five drops of Chanel No. 5" and nothing else in bed. "I don't want to say nude,"* she said, *"but it's the truth..."*

We may never know when she said that phrase for the first time (April 7, 1952, Marilyn Monroe is twenty-six years old for the first time Life Magazine featured her on the cover). That is when Chanel No5 was born.

Even though Marilyn never starred any of Chanel's campaign during her lifetime, 51 years later, she's the face of remarkable Chanel No.5 scent. Marilyn's favorite bedtime scent led to be the face of Chanel's latest campaign even after her death.

In a recent press release, Chanel describes the late cinema icon as *"the most desirable woman of the 20th century!"* Citing Monroe's famous remark from 1952 - that she wore nothing to bed but Chanel No.5 as the incentive for choosing her to front the campaign. The French house recently unearthed a recording from 1960 of Monroe "spontaneously," confirming the quote in an interview with Marie Claire.

"Although she did not appear in ads for Chanel No. 5 during her lifetime, Marilyn might be perfume's best-known ambassador. And now, more than five decades later, Chanel is tapping into its most famous fan by featuring her in an ad campaign for the fragrance."

"Chanel's new film relives the moment Hollywood legend Marilyn Monroe spoke about her love affair with Chanel No. 5." Screen icon Brad Pitt's starring role for Chanel No.5

Unique footage speaks of how Monroe fell in love with its *"best-selling perfume in front of the world, giving Chanel No.5 iconic scent status."*

George Cukor starring Yves Montand on October 12, *"Chanel procures the recording of this interview, for the first time we hear Marilyn discussing those legendary drops of No 5...you know they ask you questions, just an example, what do you wear to bed, a pajama top? The bottoms of the pajama. A nightgown, so I said Chanel No five because it's the truth, 'Marilyn then laughs' and yet I don't want to say nude you know, but it's the truth"* - The famous seductive blonde actress perfectly represents femininity which reflects in her favorite perfume, Chanel No.5

The campaign will feature Marilyn Monroe holding the Chanel No. 5 perfume in an archival photo by Ed Feingersh this November. The famous seductive blonde actress perfectly represents femininity which reflects in her favorite perfume, Chanel No.5

"Coco Chanel gave us the most famous perfume, Chanel No 5. The perfume was launched in 1921 and had its place in history secured when Marilyn Monroe was asked what she wore to bed."

Brad Pitt & Chanel

Brad Pitt's starring as a Spokesmodel role for Chanel No.5 seductively saying to the camera: "... *It's not a journey, every journey ends but we go on, the world turns, and we turn with it, plans disappear, dreams take over, but wherever I go there, you are. With luck, my fate, my fortune Chanel No 5* **INEVITABLE...**"

Coco Chanel herself was also raised in an orphanage and taught to sing- something in common with Marilyn…

Coco Chanel states, *"We think very much that the perfume is a seduction between a man, a woman, and the perfume. No.5 is our leading fragrance, and we are willing to invest in keeping it on that level."*

The product was released with ample time to sink into the psyche of both men and women. Industry reports have Pitt raking in around $7 million for the Chanel endorsement. After all, it is the first time a man will represent the luxury scent in its 92-year history. **"Her Lips Were Sealed Until Now!**

Famous Unforgettable Quotes

"I don't want to make money; I just want to be wonderful."

"No one ever told me I was pretty when I was a little girl. All little girls should be told they're pretty, even if they aren't."

"If you can make a girl laugh, you can make her do anything."

"Hollywood is a place where they'll pay you a thousand dollars for a kiss and fifty cents for your soul" Marilyn Monroe

Let's Here From Marilyn's Fans: What makes Marilyn an Icon decades later?

" It was probably her sexiness; sex sales and she had a lot of it" R.A.S

"Gee, wonder what to get sis Nina for Christmas other than the MM clock and three books?" K.A.

"What doesn't?!?! She is one of a kind!! There will NEVER be another human like her, on so many levels!" - K.R.

"Marilyn will forever remain the sexiest heartbeat in Hollywood." Says, Investigative Journalist and Author -Tammy Atencio.

"She was a star but had no one to really protect her. I feel like she always trusted the wrong people." - M.J.

"It's true, we do remember her beauty, but individually we each know how she made me feel, I love watching her movies, they still impact me." – Sheila Oliver

"Everything." - T.B.

"Her warmth, beauty strength...she believed she could...so she did" - T.A.

"Her beauty, charm, she made herself. I have three books on her." - N.A.

"Her beauty." - R.R.

"Her Insights on politics and sensuality is Timeless." - G.P.

"She was beautiful, inside and out, and she remained kind in a world that treated her terribly." - L.W.

"Hard to narrow it down; She was the epitome of a STAR. But from all I've read, she remained humble and insecure. Somewhere along the way, you can see in her a change; she discovered how powerful she was. And that is likely why she was murdered." - .B.B.

"Her beauty! No woman in these days has ever come close." - .D.S.

"She was smart and intelligent, a survivalist, innocent. Her personality and inner and outer beauty." C.S.

*"Her life is what is so ethereal, even though she was a torched soul. Wherever she is, I hope she knows how much she is loved...like they say, they won't remember what you say or do, they

will remember how you make someone FEEL. She was an expert at that. She shared her beauty with us all, as well as many very real down to earth emotions." - Sheila Oliver

"It must be somewhere in my early childhood that I first saw her in a movie. I was like enchanted from that moment on. Never before I saw a prettier face like that again, pure beauty, a kind of innocence in her eyes, and the sexiest woman ever lived! She has a glow like an angel when I look at her.

And even now, it's almost 2020, I still absorb everything I see and read about her, sometimes sad life story. She is so present in my life and in my heart. She is in heaven now and I hope she is so proud to see that so many people still love her and thinking about her and want to find out the truth about the last sad period of her life." - Barbara Bos

ATTACHMENTS

Gladys Rasmussen, Marilyn Monroe's Hair Stylist, Gladys said: *"Her hair is so curly naturally that to build a coiffure for her I have to first to give her a straight permanent... The way we got her shade of platinum is with my own secret blend of sparkling silver bleach plus twenty-volume peroxide and a secret formula of silver platinum to take the yellow out".*

In an interview in 1952, Marilyn wore *"…five drops of Chanel No. 5"* and nothing else in bed. *"I don't want to say nude,"* she said, *"but it's the truth…"*

SUMMARY

We have presented the reader with facts, backed-up with official documents to corroborate our findings. Including the night, the homicide against Marilyn Monroe occurred – vile and troublesome. Also included are the facts related to Marilyn's upbringing and portions of her life in different eras. Sometimes things come around to a complete circle. Alpha & Omega – the Beginning and the End- Our deep state is not a theory but rather a real phenomenon we experience every day – both known and unknown! We have what we believe in; sometimes, it's not tangible but rather an inner feeling that is so strong, we believe – we believe because it feels right and sets our soul at ease.

Marilyn was a kind, gentle soul who got caught up in the mix of Hollywood, where she was used by men as a sex toy – We guess some things never change.

The two authors are Californian natives. Spending much time in Malibu, and enjoyed visiting many locations where Marilyn left her prints; we are all part of Marilyn Monroe – a beam of light from one person to another; in the field of matter…we all matter! Included are a few very heart-touching comments from her fans. Marilyn was personable in character and would've loved to have kept in touch with her fans from around the world; in many ways, she has. Each reader has their own feelings about Marilyn and transcends their personal frame of mind about her.

This book will forever remain in the Loving Memory of Marilyn Monroe.
"Hold a Good Thought for Me" – Marilyn Monroe

CHAPTER 14

Some Extra Reading for your Pleasure - The JFK Assassination
Fictional in part – however, true stories inspired this writing:

Who killed JFK? As we mentioned in the previous chapters, President Kennedy made a shit load of enemies; including the CIA (was going to disband the CIA after the Bay-of-Pigs debacle), the FBI (JFK told J. Edgar Hoover to retire in 1964) and the Mafia (Sam Giancana helped JFK get elected, then both JFK and RFK turned against the MOB) also, as we put it, the MOB and the CIA were in bed together as a result of retired FBI and CIA agent Robert Maheu; and we can't rule out the Federal Reserve and the overpowering military-industrial-complex because they could have lost Millions of dollars if JFK proceeded with his plans. Renowned pathologists have said: JFK was shot from the front, not the back, also an intern medical doctor at Parkland Hospital recently said, *"...I was there, looked at the head injury and concluded that JFK was shot from the front – one of the bullets entered his right side temple and headed upwards towards the rear of his head which was blown apart at the exit wound..."*

– This would eliminate Oswald as the shooter! Here are several theories:

THEORY ONE

The Warren Commission Report, as established by LBJ, concluded that Lee Harvey Oswald was the lone shooter of three rounds that killed JFK. The question no one asked is? How can anyone shoot the FIRST TWO rounds in 1.6 seconds? You can't, the fasted and quickest it can happen is 2.4 seconds; however, all three rounds, of which the commission focused on, were done in over 6 seconds – yes, this is possible! The MSM, also known as 'Fake News,' went with this conclusion and did no investigative journalism, nor did they disclose what they learned – not much different than what is happening now, years 2016-2020, and before this!

THEORY TWO

The JFK follow car during the Dallas convoy was full of U.S. Secret Service Agents – After the first shot was heard, SS Special Agent George Hickey rose to his feet with his AR-15 and it's believed he may have shot JFK by accident or on purpose – either way, more than ten people including other SS Agents could smell the spent odor of gun powder very strong at the street level. Could this odor of gun powder have come from Agent Hickey – or the storm drain on the right side of Kennedy's vehicle when he was shot?

THEORY THREE

Our research shows, and we believe it to be true, the actual masterminds of the JFK assassination were, more likely, these four men in conjunction with the Corsican French Mobster, Antoine Guerini, as instructed by mobster Santo Trafficante?:

Allen Dulles (CIA);
David Atlee Phillips (CIA);
George H. W. Bush (CIA); and
Sam Giancana (Mafia).

Also, the following individuals were believed to be assassinated by the CIA, MOB, and Corsican French Mobster, Antoine Guerini, - MLK, RFK, John Lennon, Che Guervera, Bob Marley and many more – like Marilyn Monroe!

FBI

F.B.I. Special Agent Donald A. Adams was deeply disturbed about the JFK assassination – he wondered what went wrong by not protecting the President! The Warren Commission (inept) decided that Lee Harvey Oswald fired the fatal shot from the Texas book depository that killed JFK. However Adams said the real person responsible, not mentioned in the report; SA Adams said "…it's embarrassing because I love the FBI, it's a great organization, the best law enforcement agency in the business, but we also have to face facts, a reality, that there are bad people in this world…" (Susan Strafford, Fox 8 News - video) Adams was researching Joseph Adams Milteer – SA Adams said: *"…he was reportedly one of the most violent persons in the Country…"*

William Somersett, an FBI informant, spoke with Milteer on the phone that was bugged wherein Milteer indicated JFK would be assassinated, and the person accused of the crime will be caught within a half hour to throw the public off. Agent Adams went on to say, "…the first weapon they found in the building was a Mouser, and no one ever discussed that…" According to Agent Adams - Witnesses reported Oswald was in the lunchroom, four floors down on the opposite side of the building drinking a Coke after the first shot? So, what happened, and why didn't law enforcement uncover this? It was similar to all of the condoned hits by the government – misinformation, false exculpatory information leaked, documents fabricated, and FAKE NEWS!

CIA

It gets more convoluted:

Mrs. Harvey was interviewed by Scott and Andy Alderton at a retirement home in Indianapolis, Indiana, in 1999. JFK Facts.org PRESENTS:

According to a video recording interview, William K. Harvey served as chief of ZR-RIFLE, "D" staff , and James Jesus Angleton reported to Harvey's "D" staff, the CIA's assassination program in the early 1960's – he died in 1976; in 1999, his widow C.G. Harvey, also a CIA officer, talked about her late husband and his world. She talked about President Kennedy and First Lady Jacqueline Kennedy. C.G. Harvey said, *"…They were scum…"* also -

"…but the thing that was really upsetting, when Jack was in Rome visiting the Embassy, my husband being head of the CIA there had to assign two men along with his group of servicemen that were protecting him, and these two men were required to get the kind of prostitutes in to Jack's bed two at a time; and ah, it was a sorry thing, and my niece said now don't say that Auntie you don't know if it's true, but they were working for my husband, and they reported to

him and he told me, so I think it's true; and then while he was doing that in Rome she took off for Greece and was on the ship with Onassis, she was carrying on with Onassis, while he was carrying on with the prostitutes, I mean they were a lousy group of people, they were real scum, just like Clinton is scum..."

Now – research revealed that Mrs. Harvey was mistaken; Jackie Kennedy did travel with Onassis, but not during JFK's visit to Italy in 1963.

Mrs. Harvey about Bobby Kennedy; *"...He was an idiot, Bobby Kennedy, and my husband was absolute enemies and just pure enemies..."* About mobster Johnny Rosselli; *"... I loved Rosselli, my husband always said if I had to ride shotgun that's the guy I'd take with me, ah, much better than any of the law enforcement people; Rosselli was the kind of guy, if he gave you his desires and his friendship, well he was going to stick by it, and um, and he definitely was Mafia and he definitely was a crook, and he definitely pulled off a bunch of stunts with the Mafia, but, he was a patriot, he believed in the United States, and he knew that my husband was a patriot and that's what drew him to Bill; and he had been recruited by another guy from the FBI for assassination purposes, on Castro..."* This entire entry documented in the video interview, for your watching pleasure and additional information.

The money group who wanted him killed

(The Who, How, and Why of the JFK Assassination - Wake Up World.)

According to sources and interviews with one of Lyndon B. Johnson's mistresses, Madeleine Brown, who was also allegedly the mother of LBJ's illegitimate son, the night before the JFK assassination, a group of men gathered at the house of Dallas oilman Clint Murchison. And she was there to pick up LBJ. When he exited the building, Madeleine quotes LBJ as saying, as he left that fateful meeting, that *"...after tomorrow those SOBs will never embarrass me again. That's no threat – that's a promise..."*

Many of the alleged conspirators were among them which included:

Clint Murchison, who stood to lose a fortune if Kennedy changed the oil depletion allowance;

Haroldson Lafayette Hunt, Texas oil tycoon, same as Murchison;

FBI Director J. Edgar Hoover, who had allegedly invested millions into Murchison's oil business, and also believed that Kennedy wanted to replace him;

Vice-president LBJ – were his past ordered murders about to be found out before the JFK assassination;

Texas Governor John Connally;

Dallas Mayor, Earle Cabell (brother of CIA Deputy Director Charles Cabell -Kennedy fired him);

Richard Nixon, who had lost the election to JFK;

The Brown Brothers, of Brown Brothers/Harriman, who were involved along with the Bushes in funding the Nazis;

Joseph Sevilla, head of the Dallas mafia;

John McCloy, Chase-Manhattan Bank, a confirmed Nazi who shared a box with Hitler in the 1936 Olympic Games;

Carlos Moncello, Mafia don;

Jack Ruby (Rubinstein), who killed the patsy Lee Harvey Oswald and also who worked for Mafia boss Sam Giancana;

Malcolm Wallace, a rifle marksman, serial killer, and he allegedly made many hits for LBJ – ironically, his fingerprints, found on the weapon, in the Texas School Book Depository.

Then we have the confession of CIA Agent Everette Howard Hunt (code name Edwardo,) the mastermind of Operation 40; most all were involved in the JFK assassination and Watergate incident. Hunt named CIA operatives Cord Meyer (whose wife was apparently having an affair with JFK and go between the MOB and CIA), David Morales, William Harvey "D" staff, Frank Fiorini (Sturgis,) Bernard Barker, Dallas Sheriff Bill Decker, Dallas Police Chief George Lumpkin, and presidential limousine driver SS Agent William Greer, the secret service agent who slowed down and brought the limousine to a stop after the first shot was fired. The video available to the public was doctored to make JFK's limo seem as though it never slowed down. This slowing or stopping of the vehicle allowed the sniper from the storm drain to complete the JFK assassination.

The following persons were believed to be in the described buildings the day of the assassination:

The following persons are believed to be CIA Operation 40, heavily involved in the JFK assassination.

Dal-Tex Building

George Bush was in this building or standing outside.

The men on the 2nd floor were:

Chucky Nicoletti (Chicago mafia, gunman/shooter);

Nestor Izquierdo (Operation 40, Cuban mercenary, spotter);

Johnny Roselli (the link between Chicago mob and CIA);

Texas School Book Depository Building

The men on the 6th floor were:

Eladio del Valle (Operation 40, gunman/shooter);

Hermionos de Garcia (Operation 40, exiled Cuban, spotter);

Richard Cain (Chicago mafia);

Grassy Knoll/Picket Fence Area

Frank Fiorini or "Sturgis – code name" (Operation 40) or Rosco White (Dallas police);

James Files (gunman/shooter);

Lucien Sarti (Marseilles mafia assassin, gunman/shooter);

Bernard Baker (Operation 40, Watergate burglar);

Harry Weatherford;

Roy Hargraves (Operation 40, "Umbrella Man");

Charles Harrelson;

Felipe Vidal Santiago (Operation 40, exiled Cuban, who also took the alias of Charles Morgan);

Storm Drain/Sewer – yes, the fatal shot with the projectile heading upward and hit JFK on the right side of his temple blowing off part of the back of his head!

Curtis Crayford (brought in by Jack Ruby);

Jack Allen Lawrence.

There you have it – just a bit of information related to JFK and other assassinations – you be the judge and take your pick, or not!

"THE END of the BEGINNING"

REFERENCES

FBI – FOIA VAULT

CIA – FOIA VAULT

Wikipedia

IMDb

Facebook – Marilyn Monroe Investigative Team

Plant, Tony, 2017, Pilot, Marilyn Monroe fan and researcher

Peter Lawford editorial at Craig's Big Bands & Big Names

1994 book "My Sister Marilyn."

Obituary, New York Times by Eric Pace, Dec 25, 1984

Mail Online by Daily Mail Reporter, May 27. 2012 -'They're bullies, and they treat their women like crap':

Grande, Laura, Jun 25. 2013, Book Review: Peter Lawford: The Man Who Kept the Secrets

Boyes, Malcolm, Jan 14. 1985, the Passing of Peter Lawford Rekindles Memories of the Joys

TJB, Sep 7, 2008, on Stirred Straight Up with a twist, Sadness of a Camelot Lost at People.com by Peter, Peter, Peter

Summers, Anthony, November 22, 2007, Goddess: The Secret Lives of Marilyn Monroe

Freed, David, September 24, 1985, Times Staff Writer "…Police Open the Files on Marilyn: No Bombshells…"

YouTube

"The Missing Evidence: The Death of Marilyn Monroe." (YouTube)

Allan Whitney Snyder Make-up Artist interviewed about Marilyn Monroe (YouTube)

Gladys Rasmussen, Marilyn Monroe's Hair Stylist, 1952 (YouTube)

HARDCOPY – 1992 Investigation into the death of MARILYN MONROE 1/4 (YouTube)

HARDCOPY – 1992 Investigation into the death of MARILYN MONROE 2/4 (YouTube)

HARDCOPY – 1992 Investigation into the death of MARILYN MONROE 3/4 (YouTube)

HARDCOPY – 1992 Investigation into the death of MARILYN MONROE 4/4 (YouTube)
Rare 1964 Interview with Norma Jeane's Foster Parents (YouTube)

Old Time Radio Downloads (YouTube)

Reenber, Helmer, April 24, 1954, Peter Lawford & Patricia Kennedy - Wedding Party (YouTube)

World Wide Web

https://wakeup-world.com/2015/12/03/who-how-and-why-jfk-assassination-why-it-still-matters/

https://wwwLAmorguefiles.com

https://allthatsinteresting.com/marilyn-monroe-quotes

https://medium.com/@randhawalagan/15-interesting-facts-about-coco-chanel-c968adc7fc9f

https://pursuitist.com/marilyn-monroe-for-chanel-no-5/

https://www.refinery29.com/en-us/2013/10/55609/marilyn-monroe-chanel-no-5-perfume-advert

https://www.lubbockonline.com/article/20120731/NEWS/307319750

https://socialmediarevolver.com/marilyn-monroe-is-still-hot-after-50-years-thanks-to-social-media/

https://marilyn4ever.wordpress.com/2014/04/07/marilyn-discusses-norma-jeane-and-marilyn/

http://www.bbc.com/culture/story/20160601-the-secret-diary-of-marilyn-monroe

https://en.wikipedia.org/wiki/Marilyn_Monroe

https://marilyn4ever.wordpress.com/2014/03/14/gladys-pearl-baker-monroe/

http://entertainment.howstuffworks.com/marilyn-monroe-final-years1.htm

https://www.latimes.com/archives/la-xpm-2000-feb-17-mn-65424-story.html

https://www.theguardian.com/news/2000/mar/14/guardianobituaries1

https://www.biography.com/news/marilyn-monroe-family-genealogy

https://www.julienslive.com/view-auctions/catalog/id/180/lot/83384?url=%2Fview-auctions%2Fcatalog%2Fid%2F180%3Fpage%3D2

https://bodyheightweight.com/marilyn-monroe-family/

https://www.newworldencyclopedia.org/entry/Marilyn_Monroe

https://www.hollywoodreporter.com/news/makeup-museum-showcase-makeup-marilyn-monroe-greta-garbo-1256594

https://www.dailyfreeman.com/news/years-later-marilyn-monroe-s-star-power-shines-bright/article_d8415bb6-2c97-5b01-aec3-ddd14fe2bf5f.html?fbclid=IwAR2EugmAjpgdiaqMVyao7p35qFQujfVRjjNfncIzgWbRPX021 1Pu2i1iDxU

http://fashion.telegraph.co.uk/beauty/news-features/TMG9680298/Listen-to-Marilyn-Monroe-talk-about-Chanel-No.-5.html
https://www.youtube.com/watch?v=4jOMS-xXaqc

https://www.youtube.com/watch?v=iV9x9zEjSy

www.annualsreviews.org

http://www.genealogy.com/forum/surnames/topics/hogan/4245/

https://www.findagrave.com
https://marilyn4ever.wordpress.com/2014/03/14/gladys-pearl-baker-monroe/

http://www.oocities.org/marilynmonroesplace/family.html

https://www.biography.com/news/marilyn-monroe-mother-relationship

https://entertainment.howstuffworks.com/marilyn-monroe-early-life8.htm

https://www.theatlantic.com/health/archive/2013/02/the-original-blonde-bombshell-used-actual-bleach-on-her-head/273333/

http://dariandarlingnyc.blogspot.com/2009/10/schizophrenic-blonde.html

https://marilyn4ever.wordpress.com/2014/05/10/the-blonde/

http://www.marilynmonroe.ca/camera/about/facts/voice.html

https://www.vogue.com/article/marilyn-monroe-five-things-you-didnt-know

http://www.you-books.com/book/J-R-Taraborrelli/The-Secret-Life-of-Marilyn-Monroe

www.ingramcontent.com/pod-product-compliance
Lightning Source LLC
Chambersburg PA
CBHW081454040426
42446CB00016B/3243